Invitation
The Search for God, Self and Church

A Catholic Learning Guide for Adults

Rev. Alfred McBride, O. Praem.

Revised in light of the
Catechism of the Catholic Church

Paulist National Catholic Evangelization Association
3031 Fourth Street, NE
Washington, DC 20017-1102
202-832-5022

NIHIL OBSTAT:
Reverend Isidore Dixon
Censor Deputatus

IMPRIMATUR:
Reverend Msgr. William E. Lori
Vicar General for the Archdiocese of Washington
September 29, 1994

The *nihil obstat* and *imprimatur* are official declarations that a book or pamphlet is free
of doctrinal or moral error. No implication is contained therein that those who have
granted the *nihil obstat* and the *imprimatur* agree with the content, opinions or state-
ments expressed.

ACKNOWLEDGMENTS:

English translation of the *Catechism of the Catholic Church* for the United States of
America, copyright© 1994, United States Catholic Conference, Inc.—Libreria Editrice
Vaticana, used with permission. All rights reserved.

The Scripture quotations contained herein are from the *New Revised Standard Version*
of the *Bible*, Catholic Edition, copyright 1993 by the Division of Christian Education of
the National Council of the Churches of Christ in the USA. Used by permission. All rights
reserved.

Design prepared by Automated Graphic Systems, White Plains, Md.

Drawings prepared by Robert Cunniff, Washington, D.C.

Publisher:
Rev. Kenneth Boyack, C.S.P.

ISBN: 0-918951-05-4

Manufactured in the United States of America.

CONTENTS

PREFACE

On a perfect autumn day in l979, the late Paulist Father, Alvin Illig, and I were in St. Matthew's Cathedral, Washington, DC, awaiting the arrival of Pope John Paul II. Alvin turned to me and said, "When are you going to write an adult question and answer religion text for us? We need something like that for our evangelizing ministry." "Whenever you wish," I replied.

In that moment, *Invitation* was conceived. America's chief priest evangelizer gave me the call and I responded. The material was originally published in *Share The Word* as a catechetical addition to the excellent reflections on the Sunday readings by Laurence Brett. The text was then revised and enlarged for book publication in l984.

Providentially, the tenth anniversary of *Invitation* coincides with the historic publication of the *Catechism of the Catholic Church*. This comprehensive and systematic presentation of the beliefs of Catholics is the second such major work in the church's history, the first one being published in 1566.

Father Kenneth Boyack, successor to Father Illig, asked me to revise *Invitation* in light of the new *Catechism*. I gladly agreed to his request and believe I have produced a text that is faithful to the letter and spirit of the new *Catechism*.

What does my revision entail?

1. Virtually all the introductions for each lesson are new.
2. After the introductions you will find three new questions, with answers taken from the *Catechism of the Catholic Church*.

    This means that the revised edition has 78 substantial citations from the *Catechism*.

3. All the remaining questions and answers were looked at. Some were eliminated, partly because they were not needed and partly to keep each lesson about the same size as the original.

    In a number of instances, answers were rewritten to correspond more closely to the spirit and style of the *Catechism*. In a few cases, questions were rephrased to clarify the intended point.

4. Occasionally an answer from the *Catechism* replaces one from the original text where this seemed more suitable.
5. The sequence of lessons and topics remains the same as before.
6. The auxiliary materials in the book have been updated where necessary.

    I mentioned earlier that my revision is faithful to the letter and spirit of the *Catechism*. Happily, my original text already contained many of the basic perspectives now found in the new *Catechism*. The *Catechism's* emphasis on (l) The history of salvation; (2) The generous use of Scripture; (3) Citations from the lives and writings of the saints; (4) Extensive quotations from the documents of Vatican II (The index of the *Catechism* has five pages of citations from seventeen Church councils. Four-fifths of them are from Vatican II.); (5) A personal and pastoral approach to the learning of religion; (6) An emphasis on the accepted faith and tradition of the church.

All of these elements are also found in *Invitation*—both then and now, thus demonstrating what I mean by fidelity to the spirit of the *Catechism*, as well as its letter.

Father Illig had envisioned *Invitation* as a service to all those involved in the ministry of evangelization, the Rite of Christian Initiation of Adults and the lifelong development of adult faith. The call to faith in Jesus Christ and commitment to the church, sacraments and Christian moral witness always includes a learning moment in the process.

In any love process there is a (1) falling in love; (2) a "getting to know you" phase; (3) a commitment to staying in love. Such love is always initiated by God and sustained by his grace. *Invitation* addresses these three elements in the believer's involvement with Jesus Christ, his person, message, church, sacraments and moral challenge. Of course, *Invitation's* chief contribution to this process is phase two, "getting to know you—Jesus."

This is an adult learning guide both for newcomers to the church and for cradle Catholics as well. For those who are joining us, *Invitation* is a substantial introduction to the tradition of the church. For all Catholics it is a refresher course, a review of our beliefs in a context of faith, hope and love.

It is my prayerful hope that *Invitation* achieves the goal of all catechesis, which is to inspire a living, conscious and active faith in Jesus Christ. I envision it as a text that opens the adult faith learner to an ever deeper participation in the sacraments of salvation and a stronger commitment to witness to the moral teachings of Christ and the church in a culture hungry for precisely these virtues and life enhancing goals.

A living, conscious and active faith in Jesus Christ is itself a gift of God. The *Catechism of the Catholic Church* describes this gift in this manner: "Faith is a gift of God, a supernatural virtue infused by him. 'Before this faith can be exercised, man must have the grace of God to move and assist him; he must have the interior helps of the Holy Spirit, who moves the heart and converts it to God …'" (*Catechism*, 153). Our response to God's grace is the best known way to be happy and personally fulfilled. *Invitation* is one of the paths to that goal.

Alfred mc Bride

Rev. Alfred McBride, O.Praem.

HOW TO USE INVITATION

Adults have learning needs and a learning style quite different from that of children. To begin with, adult learners are self-directed. They are used to taking active roles in their jobs and families, and are quite capable of doing this in a learning situation as well. Secondly, adults already possess a wealth of knowledge and experience. They must integrate new information with what they already know. Finally, adults are practical. They are most interested in learning that is directly relevant to their own lives.

Invitation **is a tool specifically designed for adult learners. It does this in several different ways:**

■ A person with a particular question about the Catholic faith or the Catholic Church will find at least a partial answer in *Invitation*.

■ A person who is interested in learning more about the Catholic faith in general will receive in *Invitation* a comprehensive overview of Catholic tradition and doctrine.

In particular, *Invitation* **contains many useful excerpts from the** *Catechism of the Catholic Church.*

■ People can come together in groups to discuss the issues raised by *Invitation*, and can explore their applications to their daily lives.

Use *Invitation* **as part of your parish adult education program:**

■ Hold a course called "Review of Our Catholic Faith" for interested people. Use *Invitation* as your curriculum.

■ Hold a series of forums on specific topics, such as "What Does The Church Say About Marriage?" or "A Look At The Liturgical Year" or "Good Samaritans and Prophets: Social Justice and You." Use *Invitation* as the basis for the sessions.

■ Have parish organizations or scheduled adult education classes use selected chapters of *Invitation* to supplement their programs.

Use *Invitation* **to help inactive Catholics return to the church:**

■ Invite inactive Catholics to come to your parish for a "listening night," where they can ask questions and express their concerns about the Catholic Church and the Catholic faith. Then hold a series of sharing sessions with returning Catholics, based on their input. Refer to the table of contents in *Invitation* to help you design the sessions. The following chapters have often proved useful: 1, 3, 5, 11, 12, 15, 20, 25, 26.

■ Design a formal reentry program based on the sacrament of reconciliation. Use the following chapters:

■ Design a formal reentry program based on the renewal of baptismal promises and a commitment to the church family. Use these chapters:

Use *Invitation* **as the foundation of the Rite of Christian Initiation of Adults (RCIA) in your parish. Here are two possibilities:**

■ Use all the chapters, in order, as a curriculum guide for the catechumenate period of the RCIA. The chapters provide a comprehensive overview of what Catholics believe.

■ Use selected chapters for the various periods of the RCIA:

In the pre-catechumenate:

Chapter 1 — The Human Longing for God
Chapter 3 — People of God - Body of Christ - Temple of the Spirit
Chapter 5 — The Unique Word of Holy Scripture
Chapter 25 — I Believe ... We Believe in God
Chapter 26 — Praise the Lord

In the catechumenate:

Chapter 1 — The Human Longing for God
Chapter 3 — People of God - Body of Christ - Temple of the Spirit
Chapter 5 — The Unique Word of Holy Scripture
Chapter 8 — Mysteries of Christ's Public Life
Chapter 11 — I Believe in the Holy Catholic Church
Chapter 12 — The Celebration of the Christian Mysteries
Chapter 20 — Social Justice
Chapter 25 — I Believe ... We Believe in God

In the enlightenment/purification period:

Chapter 9 — The Paschal Mystery
Chapter 20 — Social Justice
Chapter 22 — Holy Mary, Mother of God, Pray For Us
Chapter 23 — A Faith Journey Through the Liturgical Year
Chapter 24 — Death Shall Have No Dominion
Chapter 25 — I Believe ... We Believe in God
Chapter 26 — Praise the Lord

In the mystagogia period:

Chapter 1 — The Human Longing for God
Chapter 10 — Come, Holy Spirit
Chapter 15 — Forgive Me, Father
Chapter 19 — The Vocation of the Laity
Chapter 20 — Social Justice
Chapter 21 — "That They May All Be One"
Chapter 25 — I Believe. . . We Believe in God

Use *Invitation* as a resource for Directors of Religious Education to help them with sacramental preparation:

■ They can give *Invitation* to parents to help them answer their children's questions.

■ They can give *Invitation* to couples and catechists who assist in sacramental preparation. Use the following chapters:

Baptism	3, 10, 11, 14, 21, 25, 26
Reconciliation	15, 2, 10, 12, 25, 26, 8
Confirmation	13, 19, 20
Eucharist	14, 1, 3, 4, 9, 12, 13
Marriage	17, 19, 20

Parish staffs can use *Invitation* to orient people who assist in the parish liturgies:

General	23, 9
Lectors	5, 6, 7
Eucharistic Ministers	7, 9, 13

Invitation can be a pastoral resource for people who visit the sick or help with the grieving ministry — chapters 24, 9, 10, 16, 25.

Invitation can be a tool to help orient members of parish councils — chapters 26, 19, 20, 21.

Invitation can be a general reference work (or even a gift) for new catechists, to help them answer their students' questions.

Use *Invitation* as a resource for concise answers to frequently asked questions on Scripture, morals and theology. Try running these questions and answers in your parish bulletin.

LIST OF ABBREVIATIONS

Vatican Documents and Papal Encyclicals

Church	Dogmatic Constitution on the Church
CMW	The Church in the Modern World
DRF	Declaration on Religious Freedom
DV	Dogmatic Constitution on Divine Revelation (*Dei Verbum*)
Ecumenism	Decree on Ecumenism
Evangelization	Evangelization in the Modern World
Laity	Decree on the Apostolate of the Laity
Liturgy	Constitution on the Sacred Liturgy
Non-Christian Religions	Declaration on the Relationship of the Church to Non-Christian Religions
Priests	Decree on the Ministry and Life of Priests

THE HUMAN LONGING FOR GOD

God gave us minds that will never be satisfied until they know the truth. He gave us hearts that long for absolute love. These goals are attainable because God is truth and love and wants to share his life with us.

This is made possible through his son, Jesus Christ. "Father ... this is eternal life, that they may know you, the only true God, and Jesus Christ whom you have sent ... This is right and is acceptable in the sight of God our Savior, who desires everyone to be saved and to come to the knowledge of the truth ... There is no other name under heaven given among mortals by which we must be saved"—only the name of Jesus (Jn 17:3; 1 Tm 2:3; Acts 4:12).

Our faith journey to truth, joy and personal fulfillment is toward the Father, through the Son, in the Holy Spirit. "Let the hearts of those who seek the Lord rejoice" (Ps 105:3). "You have made us for yourself, O Lord, and our hearts are restless until they rest in you" (St. Augustine, *Confessions*, 1,1).

The Human Longing For God

■ A. What is our most fundamental desire?
The desire for God is written in the human heart, because man is created by God and for God; and God never ceases to draw man to himself. Only in God will he find the truth and happiness he never stops searching for (*Catechism*, 27).

■ B. Why can we say we are all basically religious?
Throughout history down to the present day, men have given expression to their quest for God in their religious beliefs and behavior: in their prayers, sacrifices, rituals, meditations, and so forth. These forms of religious expression, despite the ambiguities they often bring with them, are so universal that one may well call man a *religious being* (*Catechism*, 28).

■ C. What is it within me that opens me to God's presence and existence?
The *human person*: With his openness to truth and beauty, his sense of moral goodness, his freedom and the voice of his conscience, with his longings for the infinite and for happiness, man questions himself about God's existence. In all this he discerns signs of his spiritual soul. The soul, the "seed of eternity we bear in ourselves, irreducible to the merely material," (*CMW*, 18), can have its origin only in God (*Catechism*, 33).

---

1 What are we looking for?

We want to be happy, and we desire peace and personal fulfillment. We also seek to love and be loved.

2 Where shall we find happiness, love and peace?

We will find happiness, love and peace in Jesus, who shows us God the Father, and sends the Holy Spirit into our hearts. "He alone is my rock and my salvation, my fortress; I shall never be shaken" (Ps 62:2).

3 Can this goal be reached here, in this life?

Each of us begins to find divinely given happiness, love and peace on earth. But its fullness will come only in heaven. God's love is everlasting. "My soul is satisfied as with a rich feast" (Ps 63:5).

4   Does God want us to be happy?

The kindness of the Lord is eternal. God is ever gracious, merciful and compassionate. Jesus says, "... abide in my love. I have said these things to you so that my joy may be in you, and that your joy may be complete" (Jn 15:9,11). The psalmist writes, "The Lord ... satisfies you with good as long as you live so that your youth is renewed like the eagle's" (Ps 103:2,5).

St. Paul repeatedly speaks of the happiness that comes from being loved by God. "Rejoice in the Lord always; again I will say, Rejoice. And the peace of God, which surpasses all understanding, will guard your hearts and your minds in Christ Jesus" (Phil 4:4,7).

5   Where do we find signs of God's desire to make us happy?

We behold God's loving care in his works of creation, providence and salvation:

■ a) *Creation:* How manifold are the works of the Lord! In his wisdom and love he gives us the world and our lives as a sign of his care. God made the world for us and us for the world.

"When I look at your heavens, the work of your fingers, the moon and the stars that you have

> *The desire for God is written in the human heart.*

established; what are human beings that you are mindful of them? You have given them dominion over the works of your hands. O Lord, how majestic is your name in all the earth!" (Ps 8:3,4,6,9).

■ b) *Providence:* "The world is charged with the grandeur of God" (Gerard Manley Hopkins, *God's Grandeur*). The Lord continues to make his presence and purpose known, to bring us love, happiness and peace. Therefore, we seek God in the experiences, needs and hopes of people, all things as well as in the beauty of creation.

"Faith throws a new light on everything, manifests God's design for man's total vocation, and thus directs the mind to solutions which are fully human" (*CMW,* No. 11).

■ c) *Salvation:* God's greatest sign of his desire for our happiness is manifested in the saving work of his Son. "For God so loved the world that he gave his only Son, so that everyone who believes in him may not perish but may have eternal life" (Jn 3:16).

6   Where are we tempted to look for happiness?

We are too often tempted to try to find happiness in a world without God, seeking satisfaction in food, sex, drink, drugs, possessions and other earthly sources. Jesus cautions us to get to the heart of the matter. "Strive first for the kingdom of God and his righteousness, and all these things will be given to you as well" (Mt 6:33).

7   How can we know that true happiness is with God?

Our restlessness is a clue. Augustine writes, "You have made us for yourself, O God. Our hearts are restless until they rest in you." From the psalmist we learn that "As a deer longs for flowing streams, so my soul longs for you, O God. My soul thirsts for God, for the living God. When shall I come and behold the face of God?" (Ps 42:1,2).

8   How does God draw us to his love, happiness and peace?

God has an infinite number of ways of touching our hearts. Among these are:

■ a) *Love of truth:* God plants in all human beings a love of truth. Even a liar is not without this hunger. God uses our inborn reach for truth to draw us to him. "You will know the truth, and the truth will make you free" (Jn 8:32).

■ b) *Attraction to goodness:* God sows within us all an attraction to goodness, especially moral goodness. When we follow our inborn affinity for goodness, we follow a star that leads to the goodness of God.

■ c) *Enchantment with beauty:* God awakens in us a longing for him through the enchantment of beauty. Emerson writes, "Never lose an opportunity for seeing something beautiful. For beauty is God's handwriting—a wayside sacrament." God brings us toward him by our experience of beauty. "One thing I asked of the Lord, that will I seek after: to live in the house of the Lord all the days of my life, to behold the beauty of the Lord" (Ps 27:4).

■ d) *Human affection:* Experiencing human affection is a powerful opening to the possibility of experiencing God's love. Every act of kindness and mercy allows the possibility of meeting Christ.

> *Jesus showed us his love by his passion, death and resurrection.*

"Truly I tell you, just as you did it to one of the least of these who are members of my family, you did it to me" (Mt 25:40).

■ **e)** *The person of Jesus:* Drawing near to Jesus brings us closer to God and closer to the hope for love, happiness and peace. "Whoever has seen me has seen the Father" (Jn 14:9). "For in him the whole fullness of deity dwells bodily" (Col 2:9). Jesus draws us to him by this truth, goodness, beauty and love, manifested in his passion and resurrection.

These qualities illustrate our capacity for God, gifts which God has implanted in our nature. However, through the act of revelation and his divine plan of salvation, God calls us to the life of grace which conforms us to Christ. This calling is God's pure gift, over and above any natural capacities, elevating us to membership in God's family, making us sharers in the divine nature and a dwelling place of the Holy Spirit.

9 Therefore, where am I going?

Our human capacity for God is matched by the divine initiative. God comes to meet us to draw us to himself. We respond to this call by going to God, through Christ, in the Holy Spirit. We should be cautious not to aim for another goal, less worthy of our calling. We believe we should be aiming our sights toward God, to enter a love relationship that grants us a happiness that "No eye has seen, nor ear heard, nor the human heart conceived, what God has prepared for those who love him" (1 Cor 2:9). We cannot do any of this on our own. We need the grace of God, imparted by the Holy Spirit who forms us as children of God in Jesus Christ.

10 How does God think of us?

He thinks of each one of us as someone lovable. "Do not fear, for I have redeemed you; I have called you by name, you are mine. Because you are precious in my sight, and honored, and I love you" (Is 43:1,4). God does not think we should be afraid of him, for we need not fear one who loves

us. It is God's love that makes us lovable, above all through divine adoption in the act of salvation. Through his son Jesus, we have been saved from our sins and restored to friendship with God.

11 What kind of love does God have for us?

He loves us like true friends. "See, I have inscribed you on the palms of my hands" (Is 49:16). God loves and accepts us, with both our strong and weak points. He treats us like a friend who knows everything about us and still accepts us. At the same time God wills us to be more than we are. His grace-filled love transforms us into his adopted children in Christ his son. Jesus says, "I have called you friends. As the Father has loved me, so I have loved you; abide in my love" (Jn 15:15,9).

12 What has been God's greatest proof of love?

His greatest proof of love was in sending his Son to be our friend and redeemer. "Blessed be the God and Father of our Lord Jesus Christ, who has blessed us in Christ with every spiritual blessing in the heavenly places, just as he chose us in Christ before the foundation of the world to be holy and blameless before him in love" (Eph 1:3,4).

13 Why should we look to Jesus in our quest for identity?

We need to look to him because he shows us what it is like to be fully human. He is the way, the truth and the life. Pope John Paul II writes, "The man who wishes to understand himself thoroughly ... must with his unrest, uncertainty and even his weakness and sinfulness, with his life and death, draw near to Christ" (*Man's Redeemer*, No. 10).

14 What motivates Jesus to be near us?

He knows we cannot live without love. Life would be senseless if love were not revealed, and if we did not encounter it. Jesus stays close to us to offer each of us his inexhaustible love. This is why Jesus liked to dine with publicans and sinners, and why he wanted to be near prodigal sons and adulterous women, as well as the sick and the poor.

St. Paul felt Christ's love so close to him that he said that the Lord was inseparable from him. "Who will separate us from the love of Christ?" (Rom 8:35).

15 How did Jesus best prove his love for us?

Jesus showed us his love by his passion, death and resurrection. "No one has greater love than this, to lay down one's life for one's friends" (Jn 15:13).

"The Redemption that took place through the Cross has definitively restored his dignity to man and given back meaning to his life in the world, a meaning that was lost to a considerable extent because of sin" (*Man's Redeemer*, No. 10).

16 How does the church describe our relationship with God?

Vatican II drew a picture of being human that is based on our relationship with God. Faithful to revelation, the picture embraces the following seven qualities:

■ **a)** *Dignity:* "All things on earth should be related to man as their center and crown" (*CMW*, No. 12).

■ **b)** *Image of God:* "Sacred Scripture teaches that man was created 'to the image of God,' is

> *Every act of kindness and mercy allows the possibility of meeting Christ.*

capable of knowing and loving his Creator, and was appointed by Him as master of all earthly creatures that he might subdue them and use them to God's glory" (*CMW*, No. 12; Gn 1:26, Sir 17:3,10).

■ **c)** *Relational:* "God did not create man as a solitary. For from the beginning 'male and female he created them' (Gn 1:27). By his innermost nature man is a social being, and unless he relates himself to others he can neither live nor develop his potential" (*CMW*, No. 12).

■ **d)** *Truth Seeker:* "In fidelity to conscience, Christians are joined with the rest of men in the search for truth, and for the genuine solution to the numerous problems which arise in the life of individuals and from social relationships" (*CMW*, No. 16).

■ **e)** *Free:* "Authentic freedom is an exceptional sign of the divine image within man. For God has willed that man be left 'in the hand of his own counsel' (Sir 15:14), so that he can seek his Creator spontaneously, and come freely to utter and blissful perfection through loyalty to Him. Such a choice is personally motivated and prompted from within. It does not result from blind internal impulse nor from mere external pressure" (*CMW*, No. 17).

■ **f)** *Spiritual:* "Man is not allowed to despise his bodily life. Rather, he is obliged to regard his body as good and honorable since God has created it and will raise it up on the last day. Nevertheless, wounded by sin, man experiences rebellious stirrings in his body. But the very dignity of man postulates that man glorify God in his body and forbid it to serve the evil inclinations of his heart" (*CMW*, No. 14).

■ **g)** *Immortal:* "It is in the face of death that the riddle of human existence becomes most acute. All the endeavors of technology, though useful in the extreme, cannot calm his anxiety. Christ won this victory when He rose to life, since by His death He freed man from death. Faith arouses the hope that they have found true life with God" (*CMW*, No. 18).

THE CREATION

❝In the beginning ... God created the heavens and the earth" (Gn 1:1). The Bible begins with these solemn words. Our creeds (Apostles' and Nicene) repeat this truth.

Science has long studied the origins of the world and the human race. These studies have enriched our knowledge of the age and size of the universe, the development of life forms and the appearance of humanity. These discoveries cause us to give even greater praise to our Creator for the wisdom and learning given to the scientific community.

But there are questions beyond scientific ones. What is the meaning of our origin? Is the world governed by chance, fate or necessity—or by God? If creation comes from God's wisdom and goodness, why is there evil? Is there a way to be delivered from evil?

The first three chapters of Genesis address these questions and the truths about creation: its origin and destiny in God, its order and goodness, the vocation of humanity and finally the drama of sin and the hope of salvation. "Read in the light of Christ, within the unity of Sacred Scripture and in the living Tradition of the Church, these texts remain the principal source for catechesis on the mysteries of the 'beginning': creation, fall, and promise of salvation" (*Catechism*, 289).

The Creation

■ A. What is the link between creation and salvation?
Creation is the foundation of "all God's saving plans," the "beginning of the history of salvation" that culminates in Christ. Conversely, the mystery of Christ casts conclusive light on the mystery of creation and reveals the end for which "in the beginning God created the heavens and the earth": from the beginning, God envisaged the glory of the new creation in Christ (cf. Romans 8:18-23) (*Catechism*, 280).

■ B. Why is our teaching on creation so important?
Catechesis on creation is of major importance. It concerns the very foundations of human and Christian life: for it makes explicit the response of the Christian faith to the basic question that men of all times have asked themselves: "Where do we come from?" "Where are we going?" "What is our origin?" "What is our end?" "Where does everything that exists come from and where is it going?" The two questions, the first about the origin and the second about the end, are inseparable. They are decisive for the meaning and orientation of our life and actions (*Catechism*, 282).

■ C. Is there a purpose for creation?
We believe that God created the world according to his wisdom. It is not the product of any necessity whatever, nor of blind fate or chance. We believe that it proceeds from God's free will; he wanted to make his creatures share in his being, wisdom and goodness: "For you created all things, and by your will they existed and were created" (Rv 4:11). Therefore the Psalmist exclaims, "O Lord, how manifold are your works! In wisdom you have made them all"; and "The Lord is good to all, and his compassion is over all that he has made" (Ps 104:24, 145:9) (*Catechism*, 295).

1 **How do we know that God created the world?**

We know this because of our belief in his revelation. We also can come to know this through reason. "Created in God's image and called to know and love him, the person who seeks God discovers certain ways of coming to know him. These are also called proofs for the existence of God, not in the sense of proofs in the natural sciences, but rather in the sense of "converging and convincing arguments" which allow us to attain certainty about the truth. These "ways" of approaching God from creation have a twofold point of departure: the physical world and the human person" (*Catechism*, 31; cf. also 33-35).

2 What is revelation?

Revelation is God's communication of himself to us.

3 How is God's revelation made available to us?

Revelation is communicated to us through Scripture and tradition. "Hence there exist a close connection and communication between sacred tradition and sacred Scripture. For both of them,

> **We are body and soul, and are created in the image of God.**

flowing from the same divine wellspring, in a certain way merge into a unity and tend toward the same end" (*Dogmatic Constitution on Divine Revelation (DV)*, 9). Both make present and fruitful in the church the mystery of Christ, who promised to remain with his own "always, to the end of the age" (Mt 28:20).

4 How should we respond to revelation?
God sharing his Relationship w/ us.

We should respond to God's offer of friendship with living faith. By active faith, we accept God's love and offer our love in return. Through this dynamic faith we believe in God's word, as it is found in the Bible, and the teachings and practices of the church.

5 What does revelation tell us about creation?

The first eleven chapters of Genesis teach us that:
■ a) God created, and continues to create, the world and human beings. He did this freely, directly, without help.
■ b) God gave being to that which in no way possessed it; called it into existence out of nothing.

■ c) He chooses human beings to be his friends.
■ d) This friendship is broken by sin.

6 Did creation happen in six days?

The six days of creation in Genesis are not to be taken literally. The story is a literary device to help the audience more easily understand that there is only one God, who is Father and creator of all that is.

7 What is divine Providence?

"Creation has its own goodness and proper perfection, but it did not spring forth complete from the hands of the Creator. The universe was created 'in a state of journeying' (*in statu viae*) toward an ultimate perfection yet to be attained, to which God has destined it. We call 'divine providence' the dispositions by which God guides his creation toward this perfection" (*Catechism*, 302). "For I, the Lord your God, hold your right hand; it is I who say to you, 'Do not fear, I will help you'" (Is 41:13). "I am with you always" (Mt 28:20).

8 Who are the angels?

Angels are spiritual "messengers" for God. Their existence reminds us that there is more to creation than what we see, feel, hear or taste (cf. 2 Sm 14:17; 2 Kgs 19:35; Book of Revelation). Church teachings about the existence of angels may be found in the documents of the Fourth Lateran Council and the First Vatican Council.

9 Who are the fallen angels?

Also known as demons, devils, principalities and powers and Satan, they are angels that have rejected God of their own free wills. The story of the rebellious angels is in Revelation (12:7-9) and Isaiah (14:12ff.).
Jesus said, "I watched Satan fall from heaven like a flash of lightning" (Lk 10:18).

10 Can fallen angels affect us?

They may try to reach us to call us to evil. The church reminds us of St. Peter's words, "Discipline yourselves, keep alert. Like a roaring lion your adversary the devil prowls around, looking for someone to devour. Resist him, steadfast in your faith" (1 Pt 5:8,9).

11 What does revelation teach about the creation of humans?

We learn that God created us as material and spiritual people. The Genesis story teaches that God took clay and breathed into it the breath of life. Therefore, we are body and soul, and are created in the image of God.

12 What is the purpose of my interior qualities?

In my interior qualities I am free, intelligent and called to responsibility. "For by his interior qualities he outstrips the whole sum of mere things. He finds re-enforcement in this profound insight whenever he enters into his own heart. Man judges rightly that by his intellect he surpasses the material universe, for he shares in the light of the divine mind" (CMW, 14,15).

13 How do our bodies help us fulfill our spiritual goals?

Through our bodies each of us is linked with material creation and bears a responsibility for it. We are called to participate with God in bringing order to the earth. "Fill the earth and subdue it" (Gn 1:28). We are summoned to enjoy the world and care for it with love. Because of Christ's resurrection, our bodies will also rise from the dead. "I believe in the resurrection of the body" (Apostles' Creed). Our human nature is a unity of soul and body.

14 In what ways are we "images" of God?

We image God in five ways: By our ability to know the truth, by our capacity for choosing the good, by our freedom to act in accordance with truth and goodness, by our human dignity which is

> *Through our bodies each of us is linked with material creation and bears a responsibility for it.*

God's gift, and by being a person in communion—which means being oriented to love and care for others.

15 How do scientific theories of evolution relate to the Bible's creation story and church teaching?

"The question about the origins of the world and of man has been the object of many scientific studies which have splendidly enriched our knowledge of the age and dimensions of the cosmos, the development of life-forms and the appearance of man ... The great interest accorded to these studies is strongly stimulated by a question of another order, which goes beyond the proper domain of the natural sciences. It is not only a question of knowing when and how the universe arose physically, or when man appeared, but rather of discovering the meaning of such an origin" (Catechism, 283-284; read all of 283-289).

16 What is grace?

Grace is God's gift of his divine love and life for us, especially through the presence of the Holy Spirit in our hearts. Grace describes the Spirit's actions, which result in the practice of Christian virtues.

17 How does the Bible speak of grace?

Scripture speaks of grace as having the following properties:
■ a) Forgiveness: By grace, God forgives us our sins.
■ b) Favor: Grace is genuinely a free gift or favor of God.
■ c) Enabler: Grace causes us to love as Christ did, and to witness to him by practicing Christian virtues.

18 What is the difference between "sanctifying" and "actual" grace?

Sanctifying grace is the relationship of love God establishes with human beings through his Spirit, dwelling in our hearts. Actual, or helping, grace refers to the help that the Spirit gives us to perform acts of good will for others.

We are not to think of grace as divided, however, for it is the one Spirit who is helping us and maintaining us in love relationships.

19   What is supernatural life?

Supernatural life is the divine love and life of the Lord, graciously shared with us.

20   What is the context for understanding sin?

The reality of sin, especially original sin, is clear only in the light of divine revelation. Apart from this, sin may seem to be only a developmental flaw, a psychological weakness, a mistake or the result of an inadequate social structure. Revelation

> *S*in destroys our harmonious relationships with other human beings.

shows us that sin is an abuse of the freedom God gave us. The saving work of Jesus finally showed us how real and serious sin is, and how it destroys us.

21   What is original sin?

"The account of the fall in *Genesis* 3 uses figurative language, but affirms a primeval event, a deed that took place *at the beginning of the history of man.* Revelation gives us the certainty of faith that the whole of human history is marked by the original fault freely committed by our first parents" (*Catechism,* 390). "Original sin does not have the character of a personal fault in any of Adam's descendants. It is a deprivation of original holiness and justice, but human nature has not been totally corrupted: it is wounded in the natural powers proper to it; subject to ignorance, suffering, and the dominion of death; and inclined to sin —an inclination to evil that is called 'concupiscence' " (*Catechism,* 405).

THIS LESSON LEAVES ONE WITH A FEELING OF HOPE!

22   How does one begin to sin?

We sin when we deliberately refuse God's offer of love and life. This is expressed when we act on our human power alone, rejecting God's power. By sin and disobedience, we repudiate God's loving plan for us. By faith and obedience, we surrender to God's love and way of living.

23   What effect does sin have on us as individuals?

Sin causes disharmony within us, resulting in a break in the peace and unity that should exist between our bodies and our souls. We feel divided, naked and ashamed. Having lost our harmonious relationship with God, we lose the secure relationship with ourselves.

"Then the eyes of both were opened, and they knew that they were naked; and they sewed fig leaves together and made loincloths for themselves." Adam said to God, "I was afraid because I was naked." To this God asked, "Who told you that you were naked?" (Gn 3:7,10,11).

24   How does sin affect our relationships with our loved ones?

God made us to be concerned about other people and to be one with them. Sin destroys our harmonious relationships with other human beings. "The Lord said to Cain, 'Why are you angry?' Cain rose up against his brother Abel, and killed him" (Gn 4:6,8).

25   What is God's response to human sinfulness?

He responds with signs of love and forgiveness and a plan for our salvation. Adam and Eve were told that the head of the serpent of evil will be crushed by a savior (Gn 3:15). In the call of Abraham, the Father begins a process of salvation that will continue in the person and work of Jesus.

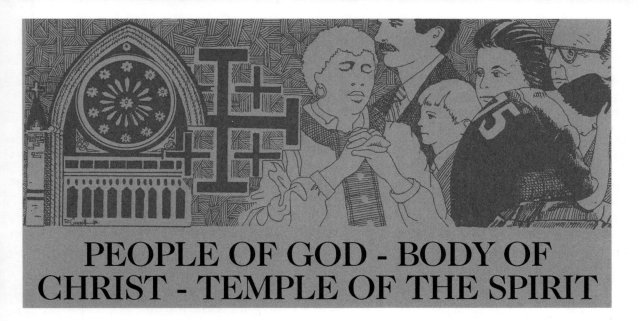

PEOPLE OF GOD - BODY OF CHRIST - TEMPLE OF THE SPIRIT

God does not touch human beings in isolation from each other, but forms them into a community to acknowledge him in truth and serve him in holiness. God chose the people of Israel as his own and nurtured them step by step in his plan of salvation.

"Christ instituted this new covenant, that is to say, the new testament, in His blood (cf. 1 Cor 11:25), by calling together a people made up of Jew and Gentile, making them one, not according to flesh but in the Spirit. This was to be the new People of God ... Established by Christ as a fellowship of life, charity, and truth, it is also used by Him as an instrument for the redemption of all, and is sent forth into the whole world as the light of the world and the salt of the earth" (cf. Mt 5:13,16) (*Dogmatic Constitution on the Church*, 9).

While our church is well known as a worldwide institution, it should also be seen as a community of love, rooted in faith in Jesus Christ and inspired by the hope of an eternal destiny in heaven. We are saved in community with one another through the Spirit of love who binds us to each other.

Three Images of Church as Community

■ **A. What are three characteristics of our church as people of God?**

♦ It is the People *of God:* God is not the property of any one people. But he acquired a people for himself from those who previously were not a people: "a chosen race, a royal priesthood, a holy nation" (1 Pt 2:9).

♦ One becomes a *member* of this people not by a physical birth, but by being "born anew," a birth "of water and the Spirit" (Jn 3:3-5), that is, by faith in Christ, and Baptism.

♦ Its *mission* is to be the salt of the earth and light of the world. This people is "a most sure seed of unity, hope, and salvation for the whole human race" (*Catechism*, 782).

■ **B. How is our church the Body of Christ?**

Christ and his Church thus together make up the "whole Christ" (*Christus totus*). The Church is one with Christ. The saints are acutely aware of this unity: "Let us rejoice then and give thanks that we have become not only Christians, but Christ himself. Do you understand and grasp, brethren, God's grace toward us? Marvel and rejoice: we have become Christ. For if he is the head, we are the members. But what does 'head and members' mean? Christ and the Church" (St. Augustine, *On John's Gospel*, 21). "About Jesus Christ and the Church, I simply know they're just one thing, and we shouldn't complicate the matter" (Joan of Arc) (*Catechism*, 795).

■ **C. What is the meaning of our church as Temple of the Spirit?**

"What the soul is to the human body, the Holy Spirit is to the Body of Christ, which is the Church" (St. Augustine, *Sermo* 267, 4: PL 38, 1231D). "To this Spirit of Christ, as an invisible principle, is to be ascribed the fact that all the parts of the body are joined one with the other and with their exalted head; for the whole Spirit of Christ is in the head, the whole Spirit is in the body, and the whole Spirit is in each of the members" (Pius XII, encyclical, *Mystici Corporis*: DS 3808). The Holy Spirit makes the Church "the temple of the living God" (2 Cor 6:16; cf. 1 Cor 3:16 - 17; Eph 2:21) (*Catechism*, 797).

---

1 **Why is community necessary in our relationship with God?**

God made us as social beings. We need one another to survive and grow, as well as to help each of us develop our relationship with God. Throughout Scripture, we see God entering the lives of individuals, only later to form them into a community.

But at a deeper and essential level, community is necessary because the love of God is poured forth into our hearts by the gift of the Holy Spirit. This love is essentially unitive. To accept the gift is to be united to the source of the gift and to all others who are accepting the same gift (cf. *Catechism*, 738).

In the Old Testament, God formed the chosen people (the Hebrews). In the New Testament, he calls his followers to unite with one another in him as a new covenant people. We continue this community today in our church. We know God as Trinity: Father, Son and Holy Spirit. God *is* community. We are called to community as part of our lives, patterned in his image.

2 Is it enough for us to feel *personally* close to Jesus?

Feeling close to Jesus is good, and very important for our faith, but it is not enough. Think of a couple in love. The most precious times are often those spent with one another. However, in order for the relationship to grow and for the individuals to develop, they must spend time with their children and other people.

Likewise, if we become satisfied with "Jesus and me" alone, we will *limit* the avenues of available communication, as well as withhold our experiences of Jesus from others.

3 What does Scripture say about living in community with God and our neighbors?

Jesus clearly calls us to develop personal relationships with him. "Come to me, all you that are weary and are carrying heavy burdens, and I will give you rest" (Mt 11:28). He also tells us, "I am the way, and the truth, and the life" (Jn 14:6).

People who know and accept the Lord are naturally drawn together because of the experience of sharing Jesus. He likens them to family: "My mother and my brothers are those who hear the word of God and do it" (Lk 8:21).

The Acts of the Apostles and the epistles describe the community developed by Jesus' early followers. Their unity and dependence upon each other are clear as they interact with the risen Jesus. The greatest punishment for early Christians was to be shut off from the community. "This punishment by the majority is enough for such a person; so now instead you should forgive and console him, so that he may not be overwhelmed by excessive sorrow. So I urge you to reaffirm your love for him" (2 Cor 2:6-8).

4 What should we keep in mind when raising our children in our faith?

As a youngster grows up, his or her faith should also grow. Ideally, the religion of our childhood should evolve into the religion of adulthood. At that time, we should personally *choose* to commit

> **W**e are saved in community with one another through the spirit of love.

ourselves once again, with deeper faith, to Jesus in the context of the church community.

In some cases, rigid, authoritarian, legalistic households can create a harsh, negative experience of the church. These circumstances can result in producing fearful, resentful, guilt-ridden adults, or even Catholics who alienate themselves entirely from the church.

Sensitive religious training, especially that which fosters prayer and virtues which will dispose the young to self-discipline, is possible and desirable within the family circle and the parish community. If care and positive reinforcement are exercised in these experiences, active church participation can become one of the happiest and most productive dimensions of a young person's life.

5 What should we do if we disagree with some of the actions of our church community?

When it comes to criticism of the community, we should recall Christ's advice that we "First take the log out of your (our) own eye, and then you will see clearly to take the speck out of your neighbor's eye" (Mt 7:5).

We should remember that we do not join a perfect group in the church community. All of us are sinners and pilgrims journeying toward better moral and spiritual goals.

At times, there may indeed be good actions taken by the community with which we do not agree. Such instances compel us to exercise patience, love and understanding. There will, no doubt, be other times when we will want the same tolerance and courtesy from others in the community.

Finally, there are some actions so based on the church's nature and mission that one could not morally disagree with them, such as the church's authoritative teachings on doctrine (i.e., the Incarnation and redemption) and morality (i.e., abortion, homosexuality and artificial contraception).

6 What causes conversion to the church?

Conversion to the church is a matter of grace and divine favor. Remember, Jesus said that we have not chosen him, but that he has chosen us. Religion is not the same as fashion or style, nor is it a matter of merely *logical* choice. It is related to the mystery of God reaching out to us and offering his divine love and salvation. We then choose, aided by the grace of the Holy Spirit, to make a faith response to the divine offer.

Most frequently we experience this offer in the context of family, loved ones, spouses or an inspiring member of the church. As Catholics, our faith response to God's call is expressed in our acceptance of the person and message of Jesus, active membership in his church, active participation in the sacraments and witnessing Christ's moral teachings in our personal lives and in the social order.

7 Why is there so much division among religions?

There are many reasons for divisions. At times they are political or historical, or they may be simply the result of a personality clash. Some divi-

> **T**he family ... has rightly been called the domestic church.

sions are based on differences in doctrine, moral teachings and interpretations of Scripture.

Christians should strive toward a real unity in Jesus, as we were instructed in the prayer, "I ask on behalf of those who will believe in me ... that they may all be one ..." (Jn 17:20,21). Ecumenism is the effort towards unity of faith. Vatican II renewed the responsibility of the church and its members to come together with other Christian brothers and sisters in one Lord, one faith and one baptism.

8 What is the church's teaching on religious liberty?

"God himself has made known to mankind the way in which men are to serve Him, and thus be saved in Christ and come to blessedness. We believe that this one true religion subsists in the catholic and apostolic Church, to which the Lord Jesus committed the duty of spreading it abroad among all men" (*Declaration on Religious Freedom (DRF)*, 1).

well formed

Each person has the *responsibility* and the *right* to determine his or her own religious activity, as long as this is done in good conscience. "On their part, all men are bound to seek the truth, especially in what concerns God and His Church, and to embrace the truth they come to know, and to hold fast to it" (*DRF*, 1).

Religious freedom should be respected. "This freedom means that all men are to be immune from coercion on the part of individuals or of social groups and of any human power, in such wise that in matters religious no one is to be forced to act in a manner contrary to his own beliefs" (*DRF*, 2).

9 How do we build up community in our religion?

Like all great gifts that come through knowing Jesus, community is the work of the Holy Spirit. At the same time, we must do our part. Make "every effort to maintain the unity of the Spirit in the bond of peace" (Eph 4:3). We receive the gift of community but we must implement it with conviction, commitment, responsibility and self-sacrifice.

The blessings of community come when we know our *own* gifts and needs, as well as those of *others*. For we are told, "There are varieties of gifts, but the same Spirit; and there are varieties of services, but the same Lord ... To each is given the manifestation of the Spirit for the common good ... that there may be no dissension within the body, but the members may have the same care for one another" (1 Cor 12:4-7,25).

10 What can we do if we do not feel we have the support of a community?

First, we can engage in an active search for community. We cannot always sit back and expect community to find us. Often, joining a small parish group, attending daily liturgy and offering our services to ministerial projects help us find community with people in our parish. In addition, prayer communities and ministerial and study groups open the benefits of community to participants.

Second, we should act in a positive manner to bring about community. St. Paul gives us good advice: "Do nothing from selfish ambition or conceit" (Phil 2:3); "Let no evil talk come out of your mouths, but only what is useful for building up" (Eph 4:29); and "Be kind to one another, tenderhearted, forgiving one another, as God in Christ has forgiven you" (Eph 4:32).

Finally, we can pray for, and be personally open to, community. The greatest responsibility we have to one another in our community of faith is our own full response to our Lord's call.

11 How is our family a community of faith?

A real community of faith can also be achieved with the members of our families. Pope Paul VI tells us that "We must not fail to draw attention to

> *All of us are sinners and pilgrims journeying toward better moral and spiritual goals.*

the role played by the family in the sphere of the apostolate which is proper to the laity. It has rightly been called the *domestic* church and this title has been confirmed by the second Vatican council ... In a family, which is conscious of this role all

the members of the family are evangelizers and are themselves evangelized. Not only will the parents impart the gospel to their children's lives. Such a family will bring the gospel to many other families and to the whole social circle to which it belongs" (*Evangelization in the Modern World*, 71).

12 What should our reaction be to those who leave the church community?

Our primary duty towards *all* community members is love and prayer. Our attitude towards those who leave the community must, however, be characterized in a very special way.

Some specific suggestions for dealing with inactive Catholics have been outlined by Father Alvin Illig, C.S.P. (*Another Look* Program) as follows:

■ a) Remember, Christ founded the church for sinners, not for angels and saints. He would have us be good shepherds, leaving the 99 who are safe to go in search of the "one who is lost."

■ b) Laity, clergy and religious must work for the spiritual renewal of the Catholic Church, especially for *personal* and *parish* renewal.

■ c) We must be willing to listen patiently to others' problems. They need to tell their story about why they have left the church.

■ d) Frequently, we must apologize for any actions that have inadvertently alienated our brothers and sisters, especially those who may have suffered indifference, insensitivity, coldness, scandal and verbal and physical abuse.

■ e) We must extend an invitation to the inactive to "come home" to the church because we *genuinely* miss them.

GOD'S INITIATIVE IN HUMAN HISTORY

THE ART OR SCIENCE OF TEACHING

The First Vatican Council taught that we can know God by the right use of our intelligence (Canon 2). But there is another order of knowledge of God that we cannot know by our own reasoning. These truths come from revelation. When we love each other we share our intimate lives with each other. God loved us so much he wished to tell us about himself in an act of revelation.

God's revelation is found in the Bible and in tradition. In this chapter we will consider Scripture's teaching about the divine plan of salvation. The Bible is a collection of many writings produced under the guidance of the Holy Spirit over many centuries. It contains a wide range of literary styles: history, biography, prayers, poetry, songs, prophecies, wisdom sayings, parables, dramas and royal chronicles.

God spoke in many voices through the talents of a variety of authors. The diversity of styles and centuries of history covered will bewilder us unless we see a pattern and unity in it all. The unifying theme of Scripture is the divine plan of salvation in Jesus Christ. God the Father loved us so much that he sent his Son to save us from sin and bring us divine life in the Holy Spirit. This is the secret of divine love revealed in the pages of Scripture. We call this plan "salvation history."

God's Initiative in Human History

■ **A. How did God unfold his loving plan for us?**
The divine plan of Revelation is realized simultaneously "by deeds and words which are intrinsically bound up with each other" (*DV*, 2) and shed light on each other. It involves a specific divine pedagogy: God communicates himself to man gradually. He prepares him to welcome by stages the supernatural Revelation that is to culminate in the person and mission of the incarnate Word, Jesus Christ.

"St. Irenaeus of Lyons repeatedly speaks of this divine pedagogy using the image of God and man becoming accustomed to one another: The Word of God dwelt in man and became the Son of man in order to accustom man to perceive God and to accustom God to dwell in man, according to the Father's pleasure" (*Against Heresies*, 3, 20) (*Catechism*, 53).

■ **B. What covenants preceded the new covenant in Christ?**
Beyond the witness to himself that God gives in created things, he manifested himself to our first parents, spoke to them and, after the fall, promised them salvation (cf. *Gen* 3:15) and offered them his covenant.

God chose Abraham and made a covenant with him and his descendants. By the covenant God formed his people and revealed his law to them through Moses. Through the prophets, he prepared them to accept the salvation destined for all humanity (*Catechism*, 70, 72).

■ **C. Why do we say Jesus is the fullness of God's revelation?**
"In giving us his Son, his only Word (for he possesses no other), he spoke everything to us at once in this sole Word—and he has no more to say ... because what he spoke before to the prophets in parts, he has now spoken all at once by giving us the All Who is His Son" (St. John of the Cross, *The Ascent of Mount Carmel*, 2, 22) (*Catechism*, 65).

1 What is the biblical meaning of God's "election"?

Election is another name for the Father's grace-filled and loving initiative in the world. His rule suffuses the world, and his favor reaches out to call specific people to witness to his will and accomplish his plan of salvation. This is first experienced in the call of Abraham (Gn 12:1ff.).

2 Are there other examples of God's election?

Other examples may be found in the selection of Jacob over Esau, of Joseph over his eleven brothers, the call of Moses, the choice of David, the birth of John the Baptist and the conversion of St. Paul.

These dramatic examples of election illustrate the broader call God makes to each human being. God "chose us in Christ before the foundation of the world to be holy and blameless before him in love" (Eph 1:4).

3 What is a consistent theme of God's election?

In the election process, God's power is always apparent. Here the humble are exalted, and life triumphs over death. "For he has looked with favor on the lowliness of his servant ... for the Mighty One has done great things for me" (Lk 1:48,49).

All examples of God's election are summarized in Jesus, who was born in humble circumstances of a virgin, caught in the bonds of suffering and death, and exalted to the right hand of the Father.

4 What is God's covenant?

The word "covenant" originated in ancient times, and referred to a contract between a powerful king and his conquered vassals. It was an agreement

> *The unifying theme of Scripture is the divine plan of salvation in Jesus Christ.*

whereby the king would protect the vassals. In turn, the people owed the king their allegiance. In the divine-human covenant, the agreement is rooted in love.

Abraham's covenant with God is with a loving father; he in turn responds with faith. Moses, representing Israel, makes a covenant with God, who is the loving ruler of his people. In turn, Israel agrees to be God's faithful people.

5 How does covenant enhance election?

Election is God's calling human beings to intimacy; covenant is the human response of faith-surrender to God's love. Abraham's faithful surrender to God is a primary example of the human reply to election, in the form of covenant. The author of the Epistle to the Hebrews cites numerous biblical examples of the covenant reply of faith to God's loving election (11:1-40).

Here we should distinguish the old and new covenants. In the old covenant, God initiated his plan of salvation and prepared the world for the incarnation of his Son. In the new covenant, "God has revealed himself fully by sending his own Son, in whom he has established his covenant for ever. The Son is his Father's definitive Word: so there will be no further Revelation after him" (*Catechism*, 73).

6 What are some concrete covenant-faith responses?

Two principal responses are worship and moral behavior. By means of worship and moral behavior, human beings reaffirm their love for God. In the Jewish covenant this was celebrated in the Passover meal, when the people remembered their delivery from slavery in Egypt and their Exodus across the sea. In all aspects of their law, they sought a moral behavior that would show their love for God.

For Christians, worship renews the covenant act of falling in love with God. We celebrate the covenant with Christ in the Eucharist, where we praise and thank God for salvation in Jesus. Moral behavior gives evidence of the desire to stay in love with God.

In the new covenant we are associated with Jesus in his perfect worship and fulfillment of his Father's will. By the grace of Christ in baptism we are a new creation in grace, which enables us to respond morally to the initiative of God in a new and more powerful way than was possible in the old covenant.

7 Who are God's People?

The Old Testament refers to the Hebrews as the People of God. In the New Testament, they are the believers in Christ. Vatican II emphasized the image of the church as People of God, to stress the community of faith aspect of Catholicism. The church is an institution, and a community, with all that implies for interpersonal love and concern (*Church*, 9-17).

8 How do humans break covenant with God?

Alongside the faith celebration in worship and moral behavior is another side of the story: the failure to love. Sin is a persistent thread in Scripture. Throughout salvation history, from the story of Adam and Eve to the idolatry of Israel, there was corruption in both the personal and the social order.

Old Testament preachers spoke against the pride of the ritualist and the selfishness of the materialist. In the New Testament, Christ's love is rejected and blasphemy is committed against the Holy Spirit (Mk 3:29).

9 How does the Bible illustrate the complexity of suffering?

As salvation history unfolds, we become more aware of the complexities of the mystery of evil, and its effects. We perceive the following:
■ a) Bad people suffer: The Bible cites numerous cases of wicked people suffering, as in the woeful end of Jezebel (1 Kgs 21:23), and the exile of the People of God.
■ b) Good people suffer: Job, an innocent and upright man, suffers material, mental, physical and spiritual anguish. In this story, we find that

> *By means of worship and moral behavior, human beings reaffirm their love for God.*

suffering purifies and matures a person. In the New Testament, stories of the healings and resurrections performed by Jesus show his will to remove the effects of sin and to save people from sin itself.

10 What is a repeated response to sinfulness?

Throughout salvation history we hear the cry of repentance, the song of conversion of heart and the confession of need for God. After his sin with Bathsheba, David prays, "According to your abundant mercy, blot out my transgressions" (Ps 51:1).

The New Testament shows the themes of moral conversion and the need for God in the stories of Mary Magdalene and St. Peter.

11 How does God's forgiveness work?

God does not show us "after-giveness"; rather, he extends "fore-giveness." The Father does not wait for us to apologize before he offers us mercy. He gives his merciful love beforehand (fore-giveness). This makes it possible for us to return to him.

There is no limit to divine love, only a limit to our ability to be open to it because we fail to believe in his love.

12 How can we know the richness of God's mercy?

We can better know God's mercy by reflecting on several historical events. For example, Noah beheld the rainbow of peace after the flood. Abraham exultantly hugged his son Isaac to his breast after God spared him. Moses and the Hebrew people marched jubilantly across the sea to freedom.

The Father's mercy also is shown in the lives of David, the prophets and John the Baptist. All of these men were heralds of the song of the angels of mercy who sang, "Glory to God in the highest heaven, and on earth peace among those whom he favors" (Lk 2:14).

13 How is the theme of messianic hope developed in Scripture?

The messianic theme was developed through two Old Testament images:
■ a) The Saving Leader: Israel experienced a series of charismatic leaders, persons touched by God. The Jews looked forward to a new savior who would have the finest qualities of past leaders such as Moses, Joshua, the Judges and King David.
■ b) The Suffering Servant: Israel also experienced profoundly holy men whose saintliness arose from acceptance of great suffering. Such was

the case of the holy martyr in Isaiah's "Songs of the Suffering Servant" (Is 42:1-4; 53).

As the true Messiah, Jesus embodied the dream of Moses where love, justice and mercy are possible. He reflected the image of David, as prophetic, poetic and prayerful; and he enfleshed the Suffering Servant by his humility, passion, death and resurrection.

14 Why are withdrawal or desert "experiences" so frequent in the biblical stories of salvation?

Withdrawal or desert experiences help the heart to respond to the guidance of God. They help us receive salvation and share it with others.

Some examples are:
■ a) Israel's 40 years in the desert before the covenant "wedding day" at Sinai.

> God does not show us "after-giveness": rather, he extends "fore-giveness."

■ b) Christ's 40-day desert fast and temptation prepared him for his proclamation of the kingdom of God.
■ c) St. Paul's time in the Arabian desert, in preparation to be a missionary. There he experienced the glory of God in the third heaven and the thorn in the flesh. The desert and the thorn would help him identify with the cross of salvation (2 Cor 12:2-9).

15 In our faith journey will all things be clear for us?

Like the cycle of day and night, we see some light, only to be plunged again into darkness. Our faith in God's grace and divinely revealed truths bring us insight, but we face times of darkness as well.

The possibilities of total fulfillment remain for us in heaven. Total clarity and fulfillment are not to be expected in this life.

16 Are there biblical stories which illustrate this future salvation?

Yes. Some of them are:
■ a) Abraham lived to see his son, but not his descendants.
■ b) Moses saw the promised land from a distance but never reached it.
■ c) Christ died on the cross. Resurrection came after death.

17 How should we respond to disappointment, suffering and death?

Christian hope is our response to life's trials. When we surrender to God in faith and love, we receive the gift of hope. This keeps our hunger for God alive, as it did for the woman at the well (Jn 4). No spiritual value is more prominent in the Bible than hope. "'Surely I am coming soon.' Amen. Come, Lord Jesus!" (Rv 22:20).

18 What are we to say to God for all his wonderful deeds?

In beholding God's plan for salvation, we can do no better than the great people of the Bible have done. We also have the example of the saints and people of good will in the church.

We can join in their chorus of praise and thanksgiving and say: "Worthy is the Lamb that was slaughtered to receive power and wealth and wisdom and might and honor and glory and blessing!" (Rv 5:12).

We are associated with Jesus in his perfect praise and thanksgiving to God for his mighty works of love. That is what the church does at the Eucharist and the Liturgy of the Hours—sung in a multitude of cathedrals, monasteries and convents, recited by clergy and laity alike.

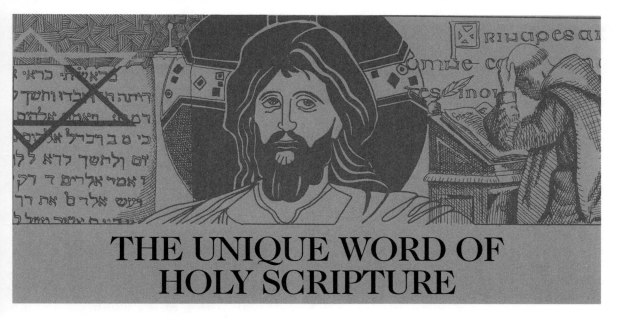

THE UNIQUE WORD OF HOLY SCRIPTURE

God speaks to us in human words. "For the words of God, expressed in human language, have been made like human discourse, just as of old the Word of the eternal Father, when he took to Himself the weak flesh of humanity, became like other men" (*DV*, 13) in all things save sin.

St. Augustine connects the word of God with the words of the Bible. "You recall that God's one word extends throughout scripture and that it resounds in the mouths of all the sacred writers, since he who was in the beginning 'God with God' has no need of separate words, for he is not subject to time" (*Commentary on Psalm 103:4*).

This is why the church has always honored the Scriptures as she honors the Lord's body. Hence we receive the bread of life taken from the one table of God's word in Scripture and from Christ's body at the altar. In our liturgies the word is proclaimed and heard to call us to faith, to form covenant with God and to prepare us to offer a sacrifice of praise.

The Unique Word of Holy Scripture

■ **A. What are the criteria for interpreting Scripture?**
l. *Be especially attentive "to the content and unity of the whole Scripture."* Different as the books which comprise it may be, Scripture is a unity by reason of the unity of God's plan, of which Christ Jesus is the center and heart, open since his Passover (cf. *Lk* 24:25-27, 44-46).
2. *Read the Scripture within "the living Tradition of the whole Church."* According to a saying of the Fathers, Sacred Scripture is written principally in the Church's heart rather than in documents and records, for the Church carries in her Tradition the living memorial of God's Word, and it is the Holy Spirit who gives her the spiritual interpretation of the Scripture ("according to the spiritual meaning which the Spirit grants to the Church") (Origen, *Hom. in Lev.* 5,5: PG 12, 454D.)

3. *Be attentive to the analogy of faith* (cf. *Rom* 12:6). By "analogy of faith" we mean the coherence of the truths of faith among themselves and within the whole plan of Revelation (*Catechism*, 112-114).

■ **B. How is God the author of Scripture?**
God is the author of Sacred Scripture because he inspired its human authors; he acts in them and by means of them. He thus gives assurance that their writings teach without error his saving truth (cf. *DV*, 11) (*Catechism*, 136).

■ **C. What is the importance of the Gospels?**
The four Gospels occupy a central place because Christ Jesus is their center (*Catechism*, 139).

1 What is the Bible?

The Bible is the inspired word of God. It is the record of God's actions in the world and a trustworthy guide for the church and its members. We know from the Bible that God created the world, and that he remains present in it. In addition, we find the story of God's people and the relationship between them and God.

One of the most valuable lessons in the Scriptures is that of human sinfulness and God's response to it with a loving plan of salvation and forgiveness.

2 What is in the Bible?

The Bible is composed of two major sections, the Old Testament and the New Testament. There are 73 separate books in all, 46 in the Old Testament and 27 in the New Testament.

A review of these books reveals a feast of literature. In Scripture we find history, poetry, songs, parables, letters, prayers, maxims, proverbs, prophecies and accounts of mystical visions.

3 How widely is the Bible known?

The Bible is the most significant book in the history of the world. As an all-time best seller, it is available in more languages than any other book. Before the invention of the printing press the Bible was copied by hand, and was accompanied by beautiful illustrations. The Bible, which means "the book," was the first book to be printed on the printing press.

4 Was there always a written Bible?

With the exception of the letters, the Bible was a spoken word before it was written down. Years ago, oral histories were a common way to preserve accounts of people's lives. Certain members of the community were entrusted with the task of remembering stories and handing them down.

A study of Scripture reveals certain "memory helps." For example, alphabetizing stanzas in poetry (Hebrew alphabet); rounding off numbers; and developing patterns for stories of honored people provide help in remembering the Bible stories.

5 How did the Bible become a written document?

Down through the centuries, the stories of the tribal elders were written down. At times, there were duplicate stories with only slight differences. Both accounts were usually written to help keep stories as complete as possible.

By the year 400 AD, biblical writings were compiled completely into one book in one language. The Bible was put into the Vulgate, which was a Latin translation of Scripture from the original languages of Greek, Hebrew and Aramaic, worked through by St. Jerome.

6 What is the difference between the Old and New Testaments?

The word "testament" means contract or covenant. The Old Testament is a series of 46 books which recount God's dealings with the Hebrews by which he nurtured their hope and expectation of a Savior and through which he pre-

pared the world for the coming of Christ. The Catholic Old Testament includes writings not "canonized" by the Hebrew people.

The New Testament contains the books of the people of the Christian covenant. The New Testament begins with the events surrounding Jesus' birth. Christians believe that both testaments are the inspired word of God. We affirm Jesus as the Messiah promised in the Old

> **R**ead the Scripture within the living tradition of the whole church.

Testament, whose saving work is outlined in the New Testament.

Christians also believe that both sections constitute one continuous account of God's plan of salvation. The words "New Testament" were first used around the year 200.

7 Can we interpret what we read in the Bible?

The Bible is like poetry in that it is always open to new and deeper meanings. People bring various experiences and backgrounds which contribute to how they understand what they read. With a positive faith outlook, people can expect to interpret it intelligently and find meaningful direction.

At the same time, individual interpretations should be measured in the light of the tradition and teachings of the church community. (cf. *Catechism*, 112-114 for the criteria for interpreting Scripture.) Meditation on the Bible has been ongoing for 2,000 years. We must guard against misinterpreting Scripture, which can cause us to miss the primary meaning of God's words, or to accept only selected sections of the Bible rather than the entire book.

8 Should we believe that the miracles mentioned in the Bible actually happened?

If we bring to the Bible a bias that miracles cannot happen, then they will be explained away as having some natural explanation. If we believe—as we should—that miracles can happen, then we will accept the biblical miracles. This is God's world and he has intervened at times in a miraculous way to love and save us.

We view the miracles of the Bible as "mighty acts of God" and manifestations of his divine love. This belief can be compared to the way we experience the miracles and mystery of daily life. The birth of a child may be explained with scientific language, or it can be viewed as God's gift, a true miracle of life.

We should view the miracles of the Bible as faith accounts of extraordinary events of salvation.

9 Why are there duplicate stories in the Bible?

The biblical events of salvation were viewed from several standpoints. Each perspective contributed an insight or aspect not noticed by other authors. Moreover, a given event is often proclaimed to a particular community in a special way in response to their faith needs.

The biblical authors wove each insight into an account of the divine plan, much like weaving a tapestry. The resulting "contradictions" are at a merely superficial level. The unity of the divine plan remains intact at a much deeper level of faith experience.

10 Why is there so much sex and violence in the Bible?

The Bible is the record of the sinfulness of people, as well as the narrative of God's love. It is therefore an account of the often stormy relationship between God and his people.

The writers of Scripture reported that God does love and forgive us for our sins. From these

> *This is God's world and he has intervened at times in a miraculous way to love and save us.*

authors we also learn that the accounts of illicit sex and violence are historical facts, not stories for our amusement or to shock us. The lesson always is the magnitude of God's grace, which far outshines the sins of mankind.

11 Are we expected to believe everything we read in the Bible?

"In Sacred Scripture, God speaks to man in a human way. To interpret Scripture correctly, the reader must be attentive to what the human authors truly wanted to affirm and to what God wanted to reveal to us by their words.

"In order to discover *the sacred author's intention*, the reader must take into account the conditions of their time and culture, the literary genres in use at that time, and the modes of feeling, speaking, and narrating then current" (*Catechism*, 109-110).

"It is the task of exegetes to work, according to these rules, toward a better understanding and explanation of the meaning of Sacred Scripture in order that their research may help the Church to form a firmer judgment. For, of course, all that has been said about the manner of interpreting Scripture is ultimately subject to the judgment of the Church which exercises the divinely conferred commission and ministry of watching over and interpreting the Word of God" (*Catechism*, 119).

12 How should we use the Bible?

We should approach the Bible with an attitude of faith and prayer. Our Lord speaks to us through the words of Scripture, and we should be open to his call. By reading the Bible as intelligent and faith-filled students, with the help of the exegetes and the guidance of the church, we can look beneath the overlays of culture in Scripture to discover the true meaning behind the texts of Scripture.

On the surface the Bible appears to be a simple story book. We should be careful, however, never to think that we completely understand it. We should take our example from the many saints and scholars who spent their lives probing the Bible in a never-ending search for an increased knowledge of the Lord.

13 Does it matter which Bible we read?

Yes, it is important for us to make a sound decision about which Bible we will use. The most obvious difference between Catholic and Protestant versions is the inclusion of several books in the Catholic Bible that have been excluded from others. These are the books of Tobit, Judith, Wisdom, Sirach, Baruch, 1 and 2 Maccabees, and parts of Daniel and Esther. Most Protestant editions include those books, but call them "apocryphal" books, meaning they are not the inspired word of God.

14 Which is the most widely used of the Catholic Bibles?

A number of good English translations are available since the discovery earlier this century of the Dead Sea Scrolls. In addition, there have been many advances in biblical and linguistic studies in recent years. The New American Bible is the latest Catholic Bible put out under the auspices of the church and recommended for use in American liturgies. It is also the most widely-quoted Bible of modern Catholic publications.

Other Catholic-approved versions include the New Revised Standard Version; the New English Bible; the Jerusalem Bible (known for its explanatory notes and cross references); and the Good News Bible (a paraphrase in easy to read modern English).

These translations are available in both Catholic and Protestant editions (which have the apocryphal books at the end).

15 Why is it important for Catholics to read the Bible?

Vatican II emphasized the importance of reading the Bible in the *Constitution on Divine Revelation*, which states, "This sacred Synod ... urges all the Christian faithful ... to learn by frequent reading of the divine Scriptures the 'excelling knowledge of Jesus Christ' (Phil 3:8). 'For ignorance of the Scriptures is ignorance of Christ.'

"Therefore, they should gladly put themselves in touch with the sacred text itself ... And let them remember that prayer should accompany the reading of sacred Scripture, so that God and man may talk together; for 'we speak to Him when we pray; we hear Him when we read the divine sayings'" (No. 25).

16 How did God inspire the authors of the Bible?

God inspired the authors of the Bible to record accurately the work of God in creating the world and saving men and women from their sins.

Under the guidance of the Holy Spirit, the biblical authors have rendered a true account of the history of salvation, the message of the prophets, the Wisdom sayings, the teachings and works of Jesus and the experiences of the first Christians.

These authors wrote from the perspective of faith and obedience to the guiding Spirit. They were loyal to the truth of God as manifested in history, human affairs and prophetic teachings.

We are called to read the Bible with a similar faith. Our hearts should be open to the guidance of the Holy Spirit in the context of church teachings.

17 What are the various meanings of the scriptural texts?

According to an ancient tradition, one can distinguish between two *senses* of Scripture: the literal and the spiritual, the latter being subdivided into the allegorical, moral, and anagogical senses. The profound concordance of the four senses guarantees all its richness to the living reading of Scripture in the Church.

> *Prayer should accompany the reading of sacred Scripture.*

The *literal sense* is the meaning conveyed by the words of Scripture and discovered by exegesis, following the rules of sound interpretation: "All other senses of Sacred Scripture are based on the literal" (St. Thomas Aquinas, *Summa*, 1,1,10).

The *spiritual sense*. Thanks to the unity of God's plan, not only the text of Scripture but also the realities and events about which it speaks can be signs.

■ 1. The *allegorical sense*. We can acquire a more profound understanding of events by recognizing their significance in Christ; thus the crossing of the Red Sea is a sign or type of Christ's victory and also of Christian Baptism.

■ 2. The *moral sense*. The events reported in Scripture ought to lead us to act justly. As St. Paul says, they were written "for our instruction" (I *Cor* 10:11).

■ 3. The *anagogical sense* (Greek: *anagoge*, "leading"). We can view realities and events in terms of their eternal significance, leading us toward our true homeland: thus the Church on earth is a sign of the heavenly Jerusalem (cf. *Rv* 21:1-22:5) (*Catechism*, 115-117).

May 9th

THE STAGES OF THE PROMISE

God uses the events of history to teach us his plan for salvation. We find a record of God's pedagogy in the 2,000 year-old salvation history of the Bible. By prayer and study we learn how God gradually prepared us for the Messiah's coming. We can discern two patterns from Israel's complex history. They are from patriarchs to covenant community and from kings to wisdom community.

The following charts capture the flow of these cycles. Read them vertically to see how each virtue is developed. Then read them horizontally to see the historical sequence. The second chart shows how the first cycle—from patriarchs to covenant community—is repeated at a new level in the second cycle—from kings to wisdom community.

Patriarchs	Slavery in Egypt	Exodus	Covenant Community
Promise of a People	Hope for a Savior	Moses	Sinai Hunger for Land/ Kingdom
FAITH	HOPE		LOVE

Kings	Slavery in Babylon	Second Exodus	Wisdom Community
Promise of Everlasting Throne	Hope for a Savior	Cyrus	Sages and Priests Hunger for Kingdom/Messiah
FAITH	HOPE		LOVE

In these lessons we perceive the spiritual nature of God's kingdom, and of the Messiah's coming. In the "slavery" deaths of Israel (in Egypt and Babylon) and risings (liberations), Jesus' death and resurrection are foretold.

The Stages of the Promise

■ A. What was the responsibility of Abraham's descendants?

In order to gather together scattered humanity God calls Abram from his country, his kindred, and his father's house (*Gen* 12:1), and makes him Abraham, that is, "the father of a multitude of nations." "In you all the nations of the earth shall be blessed" (*Gen* 17:5; 12:3; cf. *Gal* 3:8) (*Catechism,* 59).

■ B. What happened at Sinai?

After the patriarchs, God formed Israel as his people by freeing them from slavery in Egypt. He established with them the covenant of Mount Sinai and, through Moses, gave them his law so that they would recognize him and serve him as the one living and true God, the provident Father and just judge, and so that they would look for the promised Savior (cf. *DV,* 3) (*Catechism,* 62).

■ C. How did the prophets and holy women keep the promise alive?

Through the prophets, God forms his people in the hope of salvation, in the expectation of a new and everlasting Covenant intended for all, to be written on their hearts. The prophets proclaim a radical redemption of the People of God, purification from all their infidelities, a salvation which will include all the nations. Above all, the poor and humble of the Lord will bear this hope. Such holy women as Sarah, Rebecca, Rachel, Miriam, Deborah, Hannah, Judith, and Esther kept alive the hope of Israel's salvation. The purest figure among them is Mary (*Catechism,* 64).

1 What did God promise Abraham?

God promised Abraham a multitude of descendants who would be formed into a holy people. The Father said, "I will make of you a great nation" (Gn 12:2).

2 What did the Father expect of Abraham?

God expected Abraham to have trust and faith in the divine promise.

3 Why is Abraham called the father of believers?

"Faith is the assurance of things hoped for, the conviction of things not seen" (Heb 11:1). Abraham possessed this faith and inspired those who came after him to have similar faith. The author of Hebrews (ch. 11) shows how Abraham's faith in God's promises appears over and over again in sacred history.

4 How was Abraham's faith connected with hope for a Messiah?

Abraham firmly believed that God would keep his promise to be present always and to care for his people. This promise was ultimately fulfilled in the birth of the Messiah—God's son, Jesus Christ.

5 Who are the descendants of Abraham?

The immediate descendants are the people of the Hebrew covenant. However, his posterity was broadened to include others. "I have made you the ancestor of a multitude of nations" (Gn 17:5). Hence, Gentiles and Jews are to be included in the promise of God's care. God offers his promise of affection to all people.

> God offers his promise of affection to all people.

6 What does the word Messiah mean?

Messiah means "anointed one" and recalls the Jewish custom of anointing a person selected to high office, such as a priest or a king. The term also is associated with liberators or saviors. History and custom refined the word to stand for an anointed king of the dynasty of David, who would establish the kingdom of God on earth.

7 Whom did God choose as a mediator?

God chose Moses to liberate his people from the slavery of Egypt.

8 What was the Exodus?

Exodus is the name given to the first major salvation experience of the People of God. Their exodus—or exit—from Egypt into freedom was a major fulfillment of God's promise to Abraham to look after his people.

9 How did the Sinai Covenant reflect the promise made to Abraham?

God promised to create a people out of Abraham's posterity. This involved the bonding that occurred in Egyptian slave camps, as well as the glorious joy that accompanied the salvation event of the Exodus. In addition, a deepening sense of community developed during the desert marches made by the Hebrews.

At Sinai, in a covenant pact of love, God officially made Israel the people he had pledged to create. "You shall be for me a holy nation" (Ex 19:6).

10 After this, what did the Jews ask of God?

They recalled God's promise to Abraham to give them a land of their own. "I will give to you all the land of Canaan" (Gn 17:8).

11 How did the Jewish people acquire their promised land?

The Jews acquired this land through the leadership of a series of charismatic (God-inspired) leaders, called judges. These leaders began a slow, careful, military conquest of Canaan (cf. Judges; 1 and 2 Samuel).

12 Beyond hunger for a land, what else did Israel want?

The People of God strongly desired a king to lead them. The elders of Israel went to their leader Samuel and said, "Appoint for us, then, a king to govern us, like other nations" (1 Sm 8:5). Samuel, directed by God, made Saul the first king of Israel.

> **P**rophets such as Jeremiah foresaw the new covenant and a Messiah.

This concludes the first phase of sacred history. God's promise to the patriarch Abraham to deliver a land and a people is fulfilled. The process involved a period of suffering and near extinction in Egypt, followed by liberation in the Exodus and confirmation as God's people at the Sinai covenant. The Hebrew people went on to conquer Canaan and to acquire a king.

13 What did God promise King David?

God sent the prophet Nathan to King David to tell him that his throne would endure forever (2 Sm 7:7-17). This promise is vividly repeated in the psalms.

"I have found my servant David; with my holy oil I have anointed him; I have sworn by my holiness; I will not lie to David. His line shall continue forever, and his throne endure before me like the sun" (Ps 89:20,35,36).

14 What did this promise mean?

In phase one of Israel's history, the patriarchs remembered and preached God's promise of loving care for his people. In phase two, the kings of David's dynasty have the responsibility of remembering and preaching God's promise.

15 Did the kings of David's house live up to their calling?

Unfortunately, most of them did not remain faithful to their spiritual responsibilities, tending to forget the divine promise and the love agreement made in the Sinai Covenant.

16 How did the Father react to the royal infidelity of David's house?

God raised up prophets to help the people remember the promise and the covenant, and to give them hope for the future.

17 Did the prophets speak of the future?

Prophets had three duties: first, to purify the people from infidelities to the covenant; second, to read the "signs of the times" and apply the covenant vision to them; third, to awaken in God's people a hope for the future Messiah.

18 Which prophets taught about a future Messiah?

The "protoevangelium" (first gospel) of Genesis 3:9,15 is the first announcement of the Messiah and Redeemer (cf. *Catechism*, 410).

Prophets such as Jeremiah foresaw the new covenant and a Messiah. "The days are surely coming when I will make a new covenant .... I will put my law within them, and I will write it on their hearts" (Jer 31:31,33). "The days are surely coming when I will raise up for David a righteous Branch, and he shall reign as king and deal wisely" (Jer 23:5). Isaiah and other prophets took up the theme.

19 What circumstances motivated Jeremiah to look for a future Messiah?

He saw the failure of four centuries of kings to keep the covenant, and the need for a new order and new covenant.

He believed that God's fidelity would bring this about.

20 What historic event ended the Jewish monarchy?

Babylon invaded Jerusalem in 586 BC and destroyed the city and the temple, thus terminating the rule of the kings. The able-bodied people were sent into exile in Babylon. The defeated Jews were forced into labor camps, from which they worked on civic and agricultural projects.

21 Why might the return from the Babylonian Exile be called a Second Exodus?

The first liberation of the Jews from slavery in Egypt was called the Exodus (or exit) from oppression. The second liberation, from Babylonian slavery, also was freedom from an oppression, hence a Second Exodus.

When Isaiah preached to those exiled in Babylon about their imminent liberation, he used images from the first Exodus to describe the new one (Is 52:1-12).

22 Who ruled the Jewish community in Palestine after the Exile?

The throne of David was not restored after the Exile. The people remained under the rule of various outside powers, particularly the Greeks and the Romans. One exception to this was the brief period of independence under the Maccabees, from 166-63 BC.

Colonial governors ruled the political order, while Jewish priests and scholars (scribes and Pharisees) presided over the religious and cultural identity of the people. The sages, writers of the books of wisdom, served as the inspirational members of the community.

23 What were some influences on the wisdom writers?

The Jewish community was exposed to non-Jewish collections of proverbs, maxims and practical advice while in slavery in Egypt and Babylon. From the time of Solomon these collections were integrated into the religious literature of the Jewish people and reshaped by their faith outlook.

After the return from the Exile in Babylon, this wisdom literature became a special sign of the presence of God. In the past, the prophetic community had made the covenant teachings relevant to the people. Now, the wisdom community made the teachings of the people of good will relevant to the People of God.

24 How does the Suffering Servant theme connect with the Messiah?

The poems about holy martyrs or suffering servants, whose ministry would bring about justice and salvation, introduced the thought that the Messiah would suffer and die for the sake of the kingdom.

These poems apply historically to individual martyrs and to the national martyrdoms experienced in Egypt and Babylon. The Christian application of this theme to Jesus became clear mainly after the passion and death of Jesus (cf. Is 42:1-4; 50:4-10; 53:1-12; Ps 22).

25 In what ways did Jesus relive the history of Israel?

As a son of Abraham and David, he fulfilled the promise made to the Hebrews. As a savior, he repeated the saving acts of Moses, Cyrus and other liberators.

In his death and resurrection, Christ embodied the Egyptian and Babylonian and subsequent Exoduses. His passion threw light on the Suffering Servants and Holy Martyrs. As the triumphant Son of Man, he rode the clouds of the Ascension. As the Son of God, he brought an undreamed-of realization to the promise of salvation.

THE WORD BECAME FLESH

"**B**ut when the fullness of time had come, God sent his Son, born of a woman, born under the law, in order to redeem those who were under the law, so that we might receive adoption as children" (Gal 4:4-5).

"Christian, remember your dignity, and now that you share in God's own nature, do not return by sin to your former base condition. Bear in mind who is your head and of whose body you are a member. Do not forget that you have been rescued from the power of darkness and brought into the light of God's kingdom" (St. Leo the Great, *Christmas Sermon*, 1).

All the promises God made—to our first parents, Noah, Abraham, Moses, David, the prophets, the wisdom sayers—are now fulfilled in Jesus Christ, Son of Man and Son of God. In his incarnation, life, death, resurrection, sending of the Spirit and founding of the church, his saving work was accomplished and made available to us.

This loving knowledge of Jesus leads us to say our "yes" of faith in his person and message, and to share that faith with others in evangelization.

Here we meditate on the birth of the Messiah.

The Word Became Flesh

■ **A. Why did the Word become flesh?**
The Word became flesh for us *in order to save us by reconciling us with God,* who "loved us and sent his Son to be the expiation for our sins" (1 *Jn* 4:10).
　The Word became flesh *to be our model of holiness*: ..."Love one another as I have loved you" (*Jn* 15:12). This love implies an effective offering of oneself, after his example.

The Word became flesh to make us "*partakers of the divine nature*": ... "The only-begotten Son of God, wanting to make us sharers in his divinity, assumed our nature, so that he, made man, might make men gods" (St. Thomas Aquinas, *Opusc.* 57, 1-4) (*Catechism*, 457, 459, 460).

■ **B. Is Jesus partly God and partly man?**
The unique and altogether singular event of the Incarnation of the Son of God does not mean that Jesus Christ is part God and part man, nor does it imply that he is the result of a confused mixture of the divine and the human. He became truly man while remaining truly God. Jesus Christ is true God and true man. During the first centuries, the Church had to defend and clarify this truth of faith against the heresies that falsified it (*Catechism*, 464).

■ **C. What is the role of the Holy Spirit in the Incarnation?**
The mission of the Holy Spirit is always conjoined and ordered to that of the Son (cf. *Jn* 16:14-15). The Holy Spirit, "the Lord, the giver of Life," is sent to sanctify the womb of the Virgin Mary and divinely fecundate it, causing her to conceive the eternal Son of the Father in a humanity drawn from her own (*Catechism*, 485).

1 **Why does Matthew open his Gospel with Christ's family tree?**

Matthew shows that Jesus is the son of Abraham and the son of David. Thus, Jesus is clearly the fulfillment of the promises made to those two men, as well as the fulfillment of the messianic hope.

2 Why does Matthew include four "irregular" women in the genealogy lesson?

Tamar, Rahab, Ruth and the wife of Uriah represent both Gentiles and sinners. Their inclusion in the genealogy teaches that Jesus would be the savior of sinners and of Gentiles, as well as of Jews.

3 How did Matthew teach that Jesus is the Son of God?

In his family tree, Matthew teaches that Joseph is the legal, but not the biological, father of Jesus. In the story of Joseph's puzzlement over the pregnan-

> **M**atthew shows that Jesus is the son of Abraham and the son of David.

cy of Mary, an angel reveals to Joseph that the child to be born of Mary was conceived by the Holy Spirit (Mt 1:17-20).

4 How do we compare God's intervention in Christ's birth with the births of other biblical figures?

In the birth stories of Isaac, Samson and John the Baptist, God made the wombs of barren women fruitful. In these cases God cooperates with normal procreation procedures. In Jesus' birth, however, God is the absolute origin.

Being born of the Virgin Mary teaches that there is nothing in human fruitfulness that can procreate the Savior. Jesus was born "not of blood or of the will of the flesh or of the will of man, but of God" (Jn 1:13).

5 What is Matthew's broad vision of Jesus?

Matthew presents Jesus as a man, descended from Jewish patriarchs and kings. Matthew shows us Jesus as the child of the promise and thus as the Messiah. Lastly, he affirms Jesus as Son of God, born of the Virgin Mary and conceived by the Holy Spirit.

6 Why did Luke trace Christ's family tree to Adam?

In Greek, the Book of Genealogy means the Book of Genesis. Genesis tells the story of the creation of Adam. Luke sees Jesus as the second Adam, as the beginning of a new creation (cf. Rom 8:29; Lk 3:23ff.).

Also, by recalling the Adam story, Luke reminds us of God's promise of an offspring who would conquer evil: "I will put enmity between you and the woman, and between your offspring and hers; he will strike your head, and you will strike his heel" (Gn 3:15).

7 What was Luke's purpose in placing the conception and birth story of John the Baptist with that of Jesus?

God has chosen John the Baptist to be the prophetic forerunner of Jesus, preparing for the Messiah's arrival. Luke shows that even from the moment of the two conceptions the divine plan was at work. Like a true prophet, John is filled with the Spirit, even in his mother's womb. He bears witness to Jesus in the womb of Mary by leaping in Elizabeth's womb in the Visitation scene.

8 Is there a special symbolism in the angel Gabriel's appearances?

The Book of Daniel (chs. 9, 10) details Gabriel's appearance to Daniel in the temple. It is similar to the one to Zechariah in Luke's Gospel. Just as Daniel is struck dumb by the revelation (10:15), so is Zechariah (Lk 1:20). Gabriel told Daniel about the messianic times that will come in 70 weeks of years. Note the number seven, and its multiples, are symbolic for "perfect." At the perfect (or right) time, the Messiah would come.

Gabriel tells Zechariah about the birth of the forerunner of the Messiah and Mary about the birth of the Messiah himself.

9 How do Matthew and Luke use Old Testament prophecies and events to illustrate Scripture's fulfillment in Jesus?

Matthew and Luke teach the abiding, providential presence of God in history. Humans may forget God, but God never forgets them. The evangelists are not teaching that prophets foresaw the Messiah with crystal-ball clarity. Through prophecies, people before Jesus had hints and hopes about messianic times to come. But not until Christ comes do the prophecies actually become clear.

10 What was the meaning behind the angel Gabriel's "Hail Mary"?

We know from Daniel that Gabriel was the announcer of the messianic times. Gabriel's "Hail Mary" is better translated as "Rejoice, O highly favored one." This address echoes prophetic greetings to the Virgin Daughter of Israel. "Sing aloud, O daughter Zion! ... The Lord is in your midst" (Zep 3:14, 15).

"Rejoice greatly, O daughter Zion! ... Your king comes to you" (Zec 9:9). Gabriel treats Mary as the representative of Israel—Daughter of Zion. In her, God's promise to Israel would be completed.

11 Were Jewish people expecting a virgin birth?

None of the miraculous births in the Old Testament dealt with virginity. They disliked myths of virginal conceptions, which repeatedly occurred among the Greeks and Romans. The expectation was that Jewish girls would get married and have children.

Mary's virginal conception of Jesus, therefore, was a new, startling and surprising event. Indeed, it was a new creation by God. Isaiah 7:14 teaches that a virgin (or young girl), to be married to King Ahaz, would by God's blessing conceive a son in the normal manner. This is not, however, the same as Mary's truly virginal conception of Jesus by the Holy Spirit.

12 What is the meaning of the Holy Spirit's "overshadowing Mary"?

Overshadowing recalls the imagery of the luminous "cloud presence" of God that descended on the Ark and the Temple. Further, God spoke from a cloud to Jesus, James and John at the Transfiguration, as well as to Jesus, John the Baptist and the Jordan crowds during the baptism of Christ.

At the Transfiguration and at Christ's baptism, God spoke from an overshadowing cloud about Jesus being his true Son. Jesus is conceived by the Spirit's overshadowing (cloud-presence) power in the womb of Mary.

13 Luke speaks of Jesus as Mary's first born. Does this mean that she had other children?

No, it does not. First born in the biblical sense does not imply that there were other children. References to brothers were about Jesus' cousins. The same word stands for both sibling and cousin. The Catholic Church holds it as a matter of faith that Mary was always a virgin.

> *Luke sees Jesus as the second Adam, as the beginning of a new creation.*

The deepening of faith in the virginal motherhood led the Church to confess Mary's real and perpetual virginity even in the act of giving birth to the Son of God made man. In fact, Christ's birth "did not diminish his mother's virginal integrity but sanctified it" (*Church*, 57). And so the liturgy of the Church celebrates Mary as *Aeiparthenos*, the "Ever-Virgin" (*Church*, 52) (*Catechism*, 499).

14 What does Advent mean to us?

The church's liturgical season of Advent awakens us to the story of the first coming of Jesus at Bethlehem. Further, it seeks to make us aware that Jesus continues to come to the church community and to each of us, offering his saving love and forgiveness.

Lastly, Advent signals the final coming of Jesus at the close of history. At that time, the divine plan for salvation will have reached its completion.

15 How does John speak about the birth of the Messiah in his Gospel?

John reaches back and speaks of the pre-existence of the Son of God from all eternity. John writes of the Incarnation in the words, "In the beginning was the Word, and the Word was with God, and the Word was God .... And the Word became flesh and lived among us, and we have seen his glory" (Jn 1:1, 14).

16 Why does John use the Word to proclaim the pre-existence of the Son of God?

In calling the Son of God the Word, John links the Incarnation to the Genesis account of creation, in which God spoke to make the world. He also ties the event to the Word of God, which created Israel through the prophets and holy people.

The title also reflects the life-giving Wisdom Word of God, which is a "pure emanation of the glory of the Almighty" (Wis 7:25). We are led by John's portrait of the Word made flesh to a sense of awe before the mystery of the Incarnation of the Son of God. As John tells us, "God so loved the world that he gave his only Son" (Jn 3:16).

> *In calling the Son of God the Word, John links the Incarnation to the Genesis account of creation.*

17 What does Mark say about the birth of Jesus?

Mark begins his Gospel with the public life of Jesus. Therefore, he does not speak about the events surrounding Christ's birth.

18 Is Jesus really God?

In the fourth century, Arius, a priest from Alexandria, taught that Jesus was not God. He concluded that a real God would be so invisible and powerful that he would be beyond us, and therefore Jesus could not possibly be divine.

The church responded to Arius' teachings at the Council of Nicea, held in 325. It declared that Jesus truly was the Son of God. We declare our faith in Christ's divinity each Sunday in the Nicene Creed.

19 Is Jesus only human?

Nestorius was a fifth century bishop who taught that when Jesus was born of Mary, he was only a man. Therefore, Mary could not be the mother of God. Only after the birth, Nestorius said, did the child Jesus become God.

At the Council of Ephesus in 431, the church declared that the child, Jesus, born of Mary, was the son of God from his conception, as well as a man. Therefore, the Council affirmed that Mary is the mother of God. Both Arius and Nestorius were declared heretics by the church.

20 Which Council addressed Christ's real humanity ?

The Council of Chalcedon, 451, upheld the true humanity of Jesus. It taught that in Jesus there was one divine person subsisting in two natures, human and divine. Therefore, the three great Councils reaffirmed the traditional apostolic faith of the church and safeguarded Jesus' total mystery. The Councils did not create new teachings, but expressed the faith of the New Testament church in the new language of person and nature.

MYSTERIES OF CHRIST'S PUBLIC LIFE

"The whole of Christ's life was a continual teaching: his silences, his miracles, his gestures, his prayer, his love for people, his special affection for the little and the poor, his acceptance of the total sacrifice on the cross for the redemption of the world, and his resurrection are the actualization of his word and the fulfillment of revelation" (Pope John Paul II, *On Catechesis*, 9).

Jesus preached a message of salvation from all that oppresses us — above all, deliverance from sin. He inaugurated the Kingdom of heaven on earth, a kingdom of love, justice and forgiveness of sins. The church is the seed and beginning of this Kingdom. Christ entrusted the keys of the kingdom to Peter.

From the beginning of his public life, at his baptism, Jesus is the "Servant," wholly consecrated to the redemptive work that he will accomplish by the "baptism" of his Passion (*Catechism*, 565).

Christ's words and deeds reinforced each other. He practiced what he preached and he preached what he practiced. Already in his temptations in the desert, Jesus acted as messiah and savior, triumphing over Satan and demonstrating his commitment to the plan of salvation willed by his Father.

Mysteries of Christ's Public Life

■ A. What is the significance of Christ's baptism?

The baptism is the manifestation of Jesus as Messiah of Israel and son of God ... The baptism of Jesus is on his part the acceptance and inauguration of his mission as God's suffering Servant ... Already he is anticipating the "baptism" of his bloody death. Already he is coming to "fulfill all righteousness," that is, he is submitting himself entirely to his Father's will: out of love he consents to this baptism of death for the remission of our sins ... The Spirit whom Jesus possessed in fullness from his conception comes to "rest on him." Jesus will be the source of the Spirit for all mankind (*Catechism*, 536).

■ B. How did Jesus reveal the kingdom?

Jesus' invitation to enter his kingdom comes in the form of *parables,* a characteristic feature of his teaching ... Jesus accompanies his words with many "mighty works and wonders and signs," which manifest that the kingdom is present in him and attest that he was the promised Messiah ... By freeing some individuals from the earthly evils of hunger, injustice, illness, and death, Jesus performed messianic signs. Nevertheless he did not come to abolish all evils here below, but to free men from the gravest slavery, sin, which thwarts them in their vocation as God's sons and causes all forms of human bondage (cf. *Jn 6:5-15; Lk* 19:8; *Mt* 11:5; *Lk* 12:13-14, *Jn* 18:36) (*Catechism*, 546, 547, 549).

■ C. What is the link between the cross and the kingdom?

But it also recalls that "it is through many persecutions that we must enter the kingdom of God" (*Acts* 14:22): "Peter did not yet understand this when he wanted to remain with Christ on the mountain. It has been reserved for you, Peter, but for after death. For now, Jesus says: 'Go down to toil on earth, to serve on earth, to be scorned and crucified on earth. Life goes down to be killed; Bread goes down to suffer hunger; the Way goes down to be exhausted on his journey; the Spring goes down to suffer thirst; and you refuse to suffer?'" (Augustine, *Sermo* 78,6) (*Catechism*, 556).

1 What is the substance of Jesus' message?

Jesus proclaims the forgiveness of sins to all who are willing to repent, that is, to those willing to change and receive salvation (Mt 9:5,6). He also announces the arrival of the Kingdom of God, one of love, justice and mercy. It is available to those who repent of their sins and who are open to receiving this kingdom into their lives (Lk 4:16-22; Mk 1:15).

2 What is the Kingdom of God?

The Kingdom of God is the active presence of Father, Son and Spirit saving the world from sin and its effects. It is the name of a process by which God plans to achieve the victory of divine grace over evil in human affairs.

Jesus described his mission in terms of the kingdom when he said, "The Spirit of the Lord is upon me, because he has anointed me to bring good news to the poor. He has sent me to proclaim release to the captives and recovery of sight to the blind, to let the oppressed go free, to proclaim the year of the Lord's favor" (Lk 4:18,19).

3 What does Jesus teach us in the eight Beatitudes?

In the Beatitudes (Mt 5:3-12) Christ instructs us in the attitudes we need to be open to salvation in the kingdom. Pope John Paul II describes the Beatitudes as "promises from which there also indirectly flow normative indications for the moral life ... They are a sort of self-portrait of Christ" (cf. *Veritatis Splendor*, 15-16). The Beatitudes call us to discipleship and offer us empowerment in the Spirit.

4 How does the Sermon on the Mount reflect Christ's message?

The Sermon on the Mount (Mt 5-7) outlines a series of goals and ideals for Christian behavior. The sayings are a set of rules and a code of ethics, and are also guiding stars for the Christian journey. As moral principles and rules, they stretch our horizons and serve as guidelines for Christian living. If we fail in living up to them, we know we can turn to God for forgiveness, as well as for the graces to continue our journey.

5 In what way does the Last Supper Discourse fit into Christ's total message?

The Sermon on the Mount emphasized the rules and ideals of Christian behavior. The Last Supper Discourse (Jn 13-17) highlights love of God, neighbor and self as the ultimate laws of Christian morality and as the motivation for keeping the ten commandments and the rules of the Sermon on the Mount.

On the eve of his death, Jesus told us the reason for his actions. Love of God and neighbor abide as the supreme laws for Christian behavior. This love inspires every act, from humble service to willingness to die for the beloved.

Thus, as Christians we are challenged by Christ's ideals and moved to aspire to them, with the grace of God's Holy Spirit of love. This process progressively deepens our Christian attitudes, as named in the eight Beatitudes.

6 What is the role of the parables in Christ's message to us?

Jesus used stories and comparisons (parables) to express the meaning and challenge of his message about salvation and the kingdom. In doing so, he sought to correct people's misunderstanding of the

> *Jesus' invitation to enter his kingdom comes in the form of parables.*

kingdom as a worldly power. He attempted to move his listeners to appreciate the wonder, mystery and spiritual character of the kingdom.

Most importantly, he challenged people's hearts to self-knowledge in light of the demands of the kingdom. His parables invited people to be open and to accept him and his message of love (Do we allow the ideal of the Good Samaritan, Luke 10:25-37, to affect our lives? Do we truly believe in a forgiving God, as illustrated in the parable of the Prodigal Son, Luke 15:11-32?).

7 Is there anything about prayer in Jesus' message?

There are many examples of Jesus' devotion to prayer. Jesus worshipped at the Temple, celebrated Jewish religious feasts, attended synagogue and burst out joyously in spontaneous prayer (Lk 10:21). We, therefore, know that prayer penetrated his life and work.

He also "went out to the mountain to pray; and he spent the night in prayer to God" (Lk 6:12). Jesus always stayed in contact with his "Abba," his Father, whose will he constantly obeyed.

8 How does Jesus tell us to pray?

Jesus tells us to pray with confidence, persistence and attention. "Keep awake and pray" (Mk 14:38). Christ teaches us that acceptance of the message

> *Jesus tells us to pray with confidence, persistence and attention.*

means deep and long contact with the divine messenger. Above all, he instructs us how to pray in the seven petitions of the Our Father (Mt 6:9-13).

9 What does the message of Jesus demand of each of us?

In addition to the setting of high ideals, profound motivation and deep attitudes, Jesus invites us to sacrifice, to walk the way of the cross. "If any want to become my followers, let them deny themselves and take up their cross and follow me" (Mt 16:24). Jesus sets these high expectations for us, while allowing for human frailty. He stands by each of us with forgiveness for our failures and with powerful grace to enable us to live up to his hopes for us.

10 What advice does Jesus give us about our responsibility for sharing the Good News?

Jesus gives specific advice on how to act as an apostle. In Chapter 10 of Matthew's Gospel, we find a major statement which advises us to:
■ a) Bring people to say yes to the Kingdom of God.
■ b) Take time to be human, establishing trust with those we meet; "as you enter the house, greet it" (Mt 10:12).

■ c) Be prepared to suffer disappointment, betrayal and even physical abuse in the cause of the kingdom.
■ d) Trust in the power of the Holy Spirit (Mt 10:20).

11 What then are the major aspects of Christ's message?

Jesus proclaimed the Good News of our salvation from sin, and the Kingdom of God in which that salvation would be experienced. He invited us to faith in him and his message.

Christ's message is expanded in blocks (sections) of sayings. These include the Beatitudes, which teach us Christian attitudes; the Sermon on the Mount, from which we learn the Christian rules and ideals; the Last Supper Discourse, bringing the message that Christ's two laws—love of God and neighbor—are the highest moral laws and the motivation for all our actions; and the Parables, which call for personal commitment to Christ and his kingdom.

Other essential aspects of Jesus' message are found in his call to prayer, advice to missionaries and preaching on the role of the cross in discipleship.

12 How are we to respond to the message of Jesus?

Our response should include faith in Jesus and his message and a Christian behavior that spells out that faith under the authoritative guidance of the church. We must believe in the message. We must also commit ourselves to the messenger, who lays claim to our hearts and minds.

13 Did Jesus take time with people?

An unforgettable aspect of Jesus' ministry was his absorbing interest in people. Jesus was a "people" person. No one was beyond claiming his undivided, loving and compassionate attention.

He was not a loner. Rather, he was a social human being who loved being with people. He always took a genuine interest in their concerns. At the same time he devoted significant time to prayer in solitude with his Father. His prayer flowed into his ministry. His ministry flowed into his prayer.

14 Why was Jesus so interested in people?

Jesus was interested in people because he loved them and wanted to save them from the power of sin. For him there was no goal or value higher

> *Jesus was interested in people because he loved them and wanted to save them from the power of sin.*

than his saving love. On the night before he died, he dined with his best friends and talked of virtually nothing but redemptive love, salvation and union with God.

15 What are the seven signs and wonders of Jesus' ministry in John's Gospel?

In the Gospels of Matthew, Mark and Luke, healings, bread multiplications, walking on water and raisings from the dead are called <u>miracles</u>. In John they are called <u>signs</u>. The first three Gospels stress the miracles as acts of compassion. In John they keep this meaning but also serve as signs of the divine glory. St. John organized his presentation of Jesus' ministry around seven signs that together reveal the loving, saving and active presence of God in the world:
- ▪ a) The wine miracle at Cana (2:1-11);
- ▪ b) Cleansing of the Temple (2:13-25);
- ▪ c) Healing the son of the royal official (4:46-54);
- ▪ d) Curing the man at the pool of Beth-zatha (5:1-9);
- ▪ e) Multiplication of the bread and fishes (6:1-15);
- ▪ f) Cure of the blind man (9:1-7); and
- ▪ g) Resurrection of Lazarus (11:1-45).

16 What are the greatest signs and wonders of Jesus' ministry, according to John's Gospel?

For John, the cross and the Resurrection are the ultimate signs and wonders of Christ's ministry. The seven signs and wonders, mentioned above, are summed up and come to full realization in them.

If ever the glory of God was manifested and the work of the Father and Spirit made plain, it was in the great signs and wonders of salvation from sin that occurred on Good Friday and Easter Sunday.

17 Why does John emphasize the role of the faith response in each of the signs of Jesus' ministry?

The signs and wonders were events meant to awaken the experience of God in the beholders. John used the word "glory" to describe the manifestation of the Spirit.

John points out, however, that some saw and believed, while others marveled but did not believe God was present in the event. They stood before the light and love, yet remained in the darkness (and the lack of love).

18 What do we learn from John's teaching about signs and wonders?

People today are in the same position as those who drank the wine at Cana, ate the bread by the sea at Galilee or witnessed the raising of Lazarus.

For example, we are in touch with the signs and wonders of the sacraments, such as the Eucharist and the rite of reconciliation. In these events, God commands our attention and calls us to faith. Like our New Testament counterparts, we are challenged to see these events with faith and accept the salvation offered in them.

THE PASCHAL MYSTERY

The paschal mystery refers to the dying and rising of Jesus for the redemption of the world. The liturgy celebrates this, above all, in the "Sacrum Triduum" or the "Holy Three Days" of Holy Thursday, Good Friday and the Easter Vigil. On Holy Thursday, in the institution of the Eucharist, Jesus sacramentally anticipates what would happen on Good Friday and Easter.

While these celebrations are separated by time, and occurred in history on different days, they are essentially one continuous divine action. There is no Easter Sunday without a Good Friday. There is no Eucharist unless there was a Good Friday and Easter Sunday. The dying and rising of Jesus are inexorably bound together and must be viewed as one redemptive act.

In dying, Jesus conquered sin and death. In rising, Jesus brought us divine life, grace and the Holy Spirit of adoption as sons and daughters of God. We need both the negative cleansing from sin and the positive endowment of grace. In our baptism, we died to sin with Jesus and rose to divine life and grace with Jesus. The two aspects form a single reality which we call the paschal mystery.

The Paschal Mystery

■ A. How is Christ's death part of God's plan?

Jesus' violent death was not the result of chance in an unfortunate coincidence of circumstances, but is part of the mystery of God's plan, as St. Peter explains to the Jews of Jerusalem in his first sermon on Pentecost: "This Jesus [was] delivered up according to the definite plan and foreknowledge of God" (*Acts* 2:23). This Biblical language does not mean that those who handed him over were merely passive players in a scenario written in advance by God. To God, all moments of time are present in their immediacy. When therefore he establishes his eternal plan of "predestination," he includes in it each person's free response to his grace (*Catechism*, 599-600).

■ B. What is said about the witnesses to the resurrection?

Everything that happened during those Paschal days involves each of the apostles — and Peter in particular — in the building of the new era begun on Easter morning. As witnesses of the Risen One, they remain the foundation stones of his Church. The faith of the first community of believers is based on the witness of concrete men known to the Christians and for the most part still living among them. Peter and the Twelve are the primary "witnesses to his Resurrection," but they are not the only ones—Paul speaks clearly of more than five hundred persons to whom Jesus appeared on a single occasion and also of James and of all the apostles (*Catechism*, 642).

■ C. What about our resurrection?

Christ, "the first-born from the dead," (*Col* 1:18) is the principle of our own resurrection, even now by the justification of our souls (cf. *Rom* 6:4), and one day by the new life he will impart to our bodies (cf. *Rom* 8:11) (*Catechism*, 658).

1 What is Lent?

Lent is a 40-day period of time prior to Easter when the church invites us to conversion from our sins and a deeper turning toward God. It is a liturgical season which begins on Ash Wednesday, and is part of our participation in the paschal mystery, which continues in the Easter season. It is also a season in which candidates in the process of the Christian Initiation of Adults make their final preparation for initiation into the church.

2 Why do all of the evangelists record the Palm Sunday event?

The evangelists relate Palm Sunday to Christ's message about the kingdom of God and his mission to establish it. Jesus publicly began to establish his kingdom at his baptism in the Jordan. Now, on the eve of his final battle with evil, Christ makes a physical-royal entrance at the site where a spiritual-royal victory would soon take place. In making his entrance he preferred to ride the mount of the humble rulers of Israel, rather than the proud horse of the warriors (1 Kgs 1:38,5).

3 What are the major elements of the Last Supper?

The major elements found in the Gospels are:
■ a) Jesus washes the apostles' feet to call them to a ministry of humble service.
■ b) He delivers his farewell discourse, which stresses his laws of love of God and neighbor as the basis of his moral teachings and the motivation for all Christian action.
■ c) Eating the "friendship meal" in the Christian Passover emphasizes the community of love that is expected of the members of his kingdom.
■ d) The betrayal of Christ by Judas teaches us that love, which permits the beloved to be free, thereby renders one vulnerable to rejection.
■ e) Jesus institutes the Eucharist by transforming the bread and wine into his own body and blood. Speaking of his impending sacrifice and death, he says that as the bread is broken, so will his body be broken; as the wine is poured, so will his blood be shed.

His death will establish a new covenant for the forgiveness of sins. By participating in the Eucharist with faith, we share in his sacrifice and the power of his atoning death.

4 What was Vatican II's reflection on the Last Supper?

"At the Last Supper, on the night when He was betrayed, our Savior instituted the Eucharistic Sacrifice of His Body and Blood. He did this in order to perpetuate the sacrifice of the Cross throughout the centuries until He should come again, and so to entrust to His beloved spouse, the Church, a memorial of His death and resurrection: a sacrament of love, a sign of unity, a bond of charity, a paschal banquet in which Christ is consumed, the mind is filled with grace, and a pledge of future glory is given to us" (*Constitution on the Sacred Liturgy*, 47).

5 Is the agony suffered by Christ in the Garden of Gethsemane his last temptation?

Jesus faced temptation earlier in his public life, while in the desert, and later because of the urging of St. Peter (Mt 16:22-23). In his final hours at Gethsemane, Jesus is tempted to give up the cup of saving martyrdom.

"His sweat became like great drops of blood falling down on the ground" (Lk 22:44). But he reaffirmed his commitment to the Father's plan of salvation with the prayer: "Father, if you are willing, remove this cup from me; yet, not my will but yours be done" (Lk 22:42).

6 What are the wounds of Jesus' passion?

Jesus exposed himself to physical, psychological and spiritual suffering. Judas betrayed him, while Peter denied knowing him. Witnesses perjured themselves at his trial, and his best friends let him down. He suffered unjust judgments from the

> *Jesus is a wounded healer.*

Jewish high priest Caiphas and the Roman governor Pilate. Roman soldiers mocked him. He suffered agony in the garden, the scourging at the pillar, the crowning with thorns, the carrying of the cross, the nailing to the cross and the piercing of his side. On the cross, he felt spiritual desolation as he cried out, "My God, my God, why have you forsaken me?" (Mt 27:46).

7 Why did Jesus accept suffering?

Authentic love opens a person to the affection, and the affliction, of others. This was also true for Jesus. St. Athanasius says, "The unassumed is the unhealed." Therefore, the assumed can be healed.

Christ accepted suffering on behalf of sinners to remove the lust, avarice, cruelty and self-hate that cause people to do evil. In so doing, Jesus created the possibility of transforming the betrayers and deniers into persons committed to goodness and love. Jesus is a wounded healer.

This is the true and only solution to the problem of evil.

8 How does Jesus heal us in his death?

An important teaching of the Passion is that the "uncrucified is the unhealed." In assuming the malevolent death thrust upon him, Jesus heals even the deceptive teaching that death is the dark end of human strivings.

> *There is no Easter Sunday without a Good Friday.*

John's Gospel captures the victory of Christ's death in two ways. For St. John, the verb for "lifting up" on the cross is the same word he uses for exaltation. Therefore, in dying, Jesus already began to rise.

Secondly, at the moment of his death, Jesus "bowed his head and gave up his spirit" (Jn 19:30). This act of Jesus offered to the world the Breath-Spirit of life, whom Jesus promised to send.

9 Were the Jewish people to blame for Jesus' death?

Church history records numerous instances of Christians accusing the Jews for the death of our Lord. This judgment misinterpreted a line from the Passion story: "His blood be on us and on our children" (Mt 27:25).

Over the years, anti-Semites used the presumed guilt of all Jews for the death of Jesus as a reason for brutalizing them. The facts reveal that the Jewish high priest Caiphas, some hostile religious leaders and the Roman governor Pilate brought about the death of Jesus. Most Jews, however, were not part of the plot. To blame a whole people for the malice of a few is both unjust and unwarranted, as Vatican II taught in its *Declaration on the Relationship of the Church to Non-Christian Religions*.

10 What is meant by the confession made in the Apostles' Creed that Jesus "descended into hell"?

We understand by this confession that Jesus really died. The hell to which Christ went is not that of the damned; rather, it is the Old Testament con-

cept of Sheol, or a waiting place for the dead. There is little information in Scripture about the waiting process for these people. We, therefore, are unable to learn much about this experience at the waiting place (Acts 2:24-31 and 1 Pt 3:18-22). Theologian Hans Urs Von Balthasar believes that Christ's descent into hell was the ultimate expression of his self-emptying (*kenosis*), his relinquishing the status of eternal glory.

11 Where can the earliest references to Christ's resurrection be found in Scripture?

One of the earliest references to Christ's resurrection, other than the Gospels, is in St. Paul's First Letter to the Corinthians, chapter 15, verses 4-8. Here he states, "He was raised on the third day in accordance with the scriptures, and that he appeared to Cephas, then to the twelve. Then he appeared to more than five hundred brothers and sisters at one time, most of whom are still alive ... Then he appeared to James, then to all the apostles. Last of all, as to one untimely born, he appeared also to me [Paul]."

12 How central is Christ's resurrection to our faith?

The resurrection is so important to our faith that St. Paul tells us, "If Christ has not been raised, then our proclamation has been in vain and your faith has been in vain ... You are still in your sins" (1 Cor 15:14,17).

13 What are we to make of the inconsistencies in the Gospel accounts of the events of Easter?

Despite some disagreement on details, the Gospels agree on the principal elements of Easter. They all proclaim: (1) The anxiety, depression and disappointment of the apostles over Jesus' death and apparent defeat; (2) Christ's empty tomb; (3) the appearances of the risen and transformed body of Jesus to Magdalene, the apostles and other disciples; (4) the need for faith in his risen presence and the bedrock affirmation that Jesus lives and that he is risen from the dead.

14 Why did the people who saw the risen Christ have trouble recognizing him?

Christ's followers were not expecting his resurrection. In addition, Jesus now possessed a glorified body. He looked different to his friends than he had as an earth-bound being, much as the sheaf of wheat looks different from the seed from which it came (cf. 1 Cor 15:35-44).

> *A*uthentic love opens a person to the affection, and the affliction, of others. This was also true for Jesus.

Recognition of Jesus as the risen Lord requires faith in a real and objectively present Jesus: it was only when Jesus speaks to Mary Magdalene (thus calling her to faith) that she is able to recognize and acknowledge him as Lord. And, it is only when Christ breaks bread with the disciples at Emmaus (thus inviting them to faith) that their faith brings them to affirm the presence of the risen Lord.

"The hypothesis that the Resurrection was produced by the apostles' faith (or credulity) will not hold up. On the contrary their faith in the Resurrection was born, under the action of divine grace, from their direct experience of the reality of the risen Jesus" (*Catechism*, 644).

Prior to his resurrection, Jesus exercised a ministry of word, miracles and sacrament to draw others to faith. So, too, in his risen life, he performs a similar ministry. As it was for his followers who saw him, so it is for us who do not see him. Our faith is a consistent and relevant response to his saving love for us.

15 How is it that both the cross and the resurrection of Jesus constitute one saving action for us?

Through his death and resurrection, Jesus saved us. Jesus "was handed over to death for our trespasses and was raised for our justification" (Rom 4:25). By Christ's death we die to sin. By his resurrection we rise to life and adoption as sons and daughters of God by the power of the Spirit.

St. Paul preached the cross to the Corinthians and met with much resistance. But he resolutely upheld its essential importance. "The message about the cross is foolishness to those who are perishing, but to us who are being saved it is the power of God" (1 Cor 1:18).

To the Athenians, Paul preached the Resurrection, but some "scoffed," he said. To them, Paul explained that God "will have the world judged in righteousness by a man whom he has appointed, and of this he has given assurance to all by raising him from the dead" (Acts 17:32,31). The death of Jesus without resurrection is like a night without a dawn. Christ's death and resurrection form one saving act.

COME, HOLY SPIRIT

At the Last Supper Christ promised to send the Holy Spirit: "I will send him to you" (Jn 16:7). Jesus kept his promise. After his death, resurrection and ascension into heaven, he sent the Holy Spirit.

We celebrate the giving of the Spirit in our feast of Pentecost. "When the work which the Father had given the Son to do on earth (cf. Jn 17:4) was accomplished, the Holy Spirit was sent on the day of Pentecost in order that He might forever sanctify the Church" (*Church*, 4). Then, "the Church was publicly revealed to the multitude, the gospel began to spread among the nations by means of preaching" (*Decree on the Church's Missionary Activity*, 4).

The Acts of the Apostles and the New Testament epistles describe the remarkable work of the Spirit in the church. Those who believed in the Spirit became enthusiastic evangelizers, bringing Christ's message from Jerusalem to Antioch, Ephesus, Athens, Corinth and, finally, to Rome. This great missionary energy continued throughout history, so that today Christ is known and proclaimed in all nations of the world.

Come, Holy Spirit

◼ A. Why does revelation gradually unfold the mystery of Father, Son and Spirit?

"The Old Testament proclaimed the Father clearly, but the Son more obscurely. The New Testament revealed the Son and gave us a glimpse of the divinity of the Spirit. Now the Spirit dwells among us and grants us a clearer vision of himself. It was not prudent, when the divinity of the Father had not yet been confessed, to proclaim the Son openly and, when the divinity of the Son was not yet admitted, to add the Holy Spirit as an extra burden, to speak somewhat daringly ... By advancing and progressing 'from glory to glory,' the light of the Trinity will shine in ever more brilliant rays" (St. Gregory of Nazianzus, *Oratio Theol.*, 5,26) (*Catechism*, 684).

◼ B. How do we come to know the Holy Spirit?

The Church, a communion living in the faith of the apostles which she transmits, is the place where we know the Holy Spirit:
- in the Scriptures he inspired;
- in the Tradition, to which the Church Fathers are always timely witnesses;
- in the Church's Magisterium, which he assists;
- in the sacramental liturgy, through its words and symbols, in which the Holy Spirit puts us into communion with Christ;
- in prayer, wherein he intercedes for us;
- in the charisms and ministries by which the Church is built up;
- in the signs of apostolic and missionary life;
- in the witness of saints through whom he manifests his holiness and continues the work of salvation (*Catechism*, 688).

◼ C. Does the Spirit lead us to the "last days"?

By his coming, which never ceases, the Holy Spirit causes the world to enter into the "last days," the time of the Church, the Kingdom already inherited though not yet consummated (*Catechism*, 732).

1 Where does the word Pentecost come from?

Pentecost was the name of a Jewish festival occurring on the fiftieth day after Passover. The Jews celebrated the memory of God's covenant with their ancestors at Mount Sinai. Wind and fire swept the slopes of Sinai that day, symbolizing God's presence.

2 How does the meaning of the Jewish Pentecost relate to the Christian Pentecost?

The events of the upper room of the Christian Pentecost are like those of a new Sinai covenant. Once again, the mighty Breath-Spirit of God and the fire of his presence touched a community of believers. The Spirit forged a new, permanent covenant that brought about the creation of a new people of God—the church. The Law written on the heart at Pentecost is in contrast to the Law written on stone tablets, which does nothing to effect inner transformation or empower.

3 What is the purpose of the gifts of the Holy Spirit?

Jesus sends the Holy Spirit to each of us that we may become endowed with a diversity of special gifts. All the members of the church are to use their gifts in a spirit of unity to help build up the Body of Christ.

4 Where are the gifts of the Spirit to be found in Scripture?

Isaiah 11:2 lists the gifts of the Spirit that will be found in the Messiah. "The spirit of the Lord shall rest on him: the spirit of wisdom and understand-

> *The Spirit forged a new, permanent covenant that brought about the creation of a new people of God— the church.*

ing, the spirit of counsel and might, the spirit of knowledge and the fear of the Lord."

There is also a list of gifts of the Holy Spirit in 1 Corinthians 12:4-11. They are wisdom, knowledge, faith, healing, miraculous powers, prophecy, discernment, tongues and interpretation of tongues.

Traditional catechesis lists seven gifts of the Spirit as: wisdom, knowledge, understanding, courage, counsel, piety and fear of the Lord. All these gifts further our salvation and build up the church.

5 What is the greatest gift of the Holy Spirit?

Love is the greatest gift of the Spirit. This love is the basic gift from which all other gifts derive. St. Paul sings of the Spirit's gift of love in a language worthy of the richest poetry (cf. 1 Cor 13:1-13).

6 What is the purpose of the gift of tongues?

The purpose of the gift of tongues is to lead us toward building the church community of love and trust. St. Paul addressed this question. He said it is not a major gift and was not to be used to excess (cf. 1 Cor 14:27-28).

7 Does the Spirit's gift of healing still exist?

The prophet Isaiah predicted that healing would occur in messianic times. "Then the eyes of the blind shall be opened, and the ears of the deaf unstopped ..." (35:5). The Gospels reported numerous healing miracles in Christ's ministry, as was prophesied. In baptism there are rituals associated with the conferral of sight, hearing and speech.

Today, the church requires evidence of miracles for canonization to sainthood, most being miracles of healing. Lourdes is the most popular shrine of our church, a place where the Spirit's gift of healing is sought.

In a broader sense, every Christian may participate in the gift of healing. This is especially seen in the hospital ministry, in which many participate in the good work of the "healing community."

8 What is the Spirit's gift of discernment?

A case of the Spirit's gift of discernment is described in the Acts of the Apostles, chapter 15. The early church was divided by the question of whether Gentile converts should be circumcised and be compelled to adhere to Jewish dietary laws before being allowed into the church. Then, the "whole assembly kept silence" (v. 12). They prayed in silent attention to the Spirit for discernment on this issue.

After much prayer they decided to exempt Gentile converts from circumcision and dietary laws. The way was paved for the world mission to the Gentiles. The gift of discernment continues today. Vital decisions can be made using reason aided by faith and openness to the Spirit's love.

9 — What is the relationship of the Spirit to the Father and the Son?

The Holy Spirit is the bond of unity between the Father and the Son in the most Holy Trinity. Love is a person of the Trinity, the Holy Spirit. The Trinity is like a family: a Father and Son who love each other, and a Holy Spirit who is the very person of love who binds Father and Son together. That same love comes to us because "God's love has been poured into our hearts through the Holy Spirit" (Rom 5:5).

10 — How does the Spirit produce the "mind of Christ" within us?

Acting under the guidance of the Spirit, we come to see life from the viewpoint and attitudes of Christ. We experience ourselves as children of God, who is our "Abba! Father!" (Rom 8:15). Just as Jesus was led by the Spirit, so are we. Jesus is the way to the Father, and the Spirit is the way to Jesus.

11 — How does the Spirit help us to pray?

"The Spirit helps us in our weakness; for we do not know how to pray as we ought, but that very Spirit intercedes with sighs too deep for words" (Rom 8:26). "No one can say 'Jesus is Lord' except by the Holy Spirit" (1 Cor 12:3).

12 — What is the immediate effect of the Pentecost event?

The power of the Spirit moved Peter to take the leadership role over the believers in the ministry of evangelization. Made bold by the Spirit, Peter proclaimed Jesus and called for conversion to him and for the acceptance of baptism (Acts 2:14-41).

On the Mount of the Ascension, Jesus commissioned his followers to this ministry. "Go therefore and make disciples of all nations, baptizing them in the name of the Father and of the Son and of the Holy Spirit, and teaching them to obey everything that I have commanded you" (Mt 28:19-20).

13 — What is the origin of the word *evangelization*?

The word evangelization derives from the Greek term meaning "good news." In biblical and church usage, evangelization refers to an act that calls the listener to say yes to Jesus Christ. We are asked to accept Christ's gift of salvation from sin and to say yes to his kingdom of love, justice and mercy. We are then called to baptism into active membership in the church community.

14 — Who is the church's audience for evangelization?

The audience for evangelization includes the unchurched (those who have not yet accepted Christ), alienated Catholics (those who have abandoned their commitment to Jesus) and churched Catholics (those who have remained faithful to Jesus and active membership in the church).

15 — Why is it important to evangelize churched Catholics?

As churched Catholics journey through their lives, they need to be called again and again to say yes to Jesus. Stages of personal maturing should be accompanied by stages of spiritual maturing.

> *Just as Jesus was led by the Spirit, so are we.*

Evangelizing the churched Catholic is a repeated call to deepen one's love of the Lord. During liturgical seasons such as Advent and Lent, the holy days of Christmas, Easter and Pentecost and the feasts of Mary and the saints, the church continues to evangelize her community of believers.

16 — Who are those called to be missionaries for the church?

Every follower of Christ is called to witness and to proclaim Jesus to others, especially to the unchurched. In the words of St. Paul, "And woe to me if I do not proclaim the gospel!" (1 Cor 9:16).

In addition, we receive direction about missionary work from Vatican II, which teaches that "Since the whole Church is missionary, and the work of evangelization is a basic duty of the People of God ...," the obligation of sharing the faith is imposed on every disciple of Christ (*Decree on the Church's Missionary Activity*, 35).

"For the Church is compelled by the Holy Spirit to do her part towards the full realization of the will of God, who has established Christ as the source of salvation for the whole world" (*Church*, 17).

17 Can a church that does not have a missionary spirit be fully Catholic?

Commenting on the validity of the "Young Churches of Asia, Africa and Latin America," Pope John Paul II states: "These young Churches, who in their turn have become missionary, give proof of their maturity in faith. They have understood that if a particular Church is not missionary, it is not fully Catholic.

> *E*very follower of Christ is called to witness and to proclaim Jesus to others.

"A Church that is closed in upon itself, without a missionary openness, is an incomplete and 'sick Church.' The example of missionary awareness set by the young Churches should bring home this truth to older Churches ..." (Mission Sunday Message, 1981).

18 What is the missionary role of the Christian family?

Pope John Paul I outlined the missionary role of the family as follows: "Through family prayer, the 'domestic Church' becomes an effective reality and leads to the transformation of the world. All efforts of parents to instill God's love into their children and to support them by the example of their faith constitute a most relevant apostolate for the 20th Century" (Address to U.S. Bishops, Sept. 21, 1978).

19 How does the church's position on justice relate to mission work?

The church preaches Christ's message of salvation and the need to make his kingdom of love, justice and mercy real for each of us. Sin lies at the root of injustice, loveless lives and merciless behavior. There should be both a proclamation of the Gospel, and an implementing of it in the practical order.

Evangelization and missionary efforts must always concentrate on this total vision of Christ that includes both faith and good works. Workers in mission fields must look to social services, which heal the symptoms of injustice, and to social reforms, which heal the causes of injustice. Among these workers must be found good Samaritans and prophets who witness to a ministry of justice.

20 Why is cultural sensitivity essential to mission work?

Jesus should be incarnated in the various cultures and ethnic awarenesses of our time. Culturally sensitive missionaries examine the customs, traditions, wisdom, knowledge, arts and sciences of local people. This review enables young churches to integrate their ethnicity with the light of the Gospel and Catholic tradition.

I BELIEVE IN THE HOLY CATHOLIC CHURCH

"Christ is the light of all nations. Hence this most sacred Synod, which has been gathered in the Holy Spirit, eagerly desires to shed on all men that radiance of His which brightens the countenance of the Church. This it will do by proclaiming the gospel to every creature" (*Church*, 1). With these words the Fathers of the Council deliberately linked the church to Jesus, upon whom the church depends absolutely. One of the earliest names for the church is Body of Christ. Whatever light the church has flows from Jesus, the light of the world.

Secondly, the church is equally bound to the Holy Spirit who made it visible at Pentecost. As the source and giver of holiness, the Spirit endows the church with holiness. St. Hippolytus said the church is the place "where the Spirit flourishes" (*Tradition of the Apostles*, 35).

Thirdly, our belief in the marks of the church as one, holy, catholic and apostolic is essentially tied to our faith in Father, Son and Spirit. In the creed we say we believe in the church, but not in the same sense that we affirm our faith in the trinity. We distinguish God from his works. We believe in the church as the creation of God and the sacrament of salvation (effective sign of redemption) for the world.

It is Father, Son and Spirit who call into existence the holy assembly of the church. There we hear the word, celebrate the sacraments of salvation, form covenant with God and promise to witness Jesus to others.

I Believe in the Holy Catholic Church

■ **A. How do we balance our vision of the church as both visible and spiritual?**
"The one mediator, Christ, established and ever sustains here on earth his holy Church, the community of faith, hope, and charity, as a visible organization through

which he communicates truth and grace to all men" (*LG* 8 § 1). The Church is at the same time:
- a "society structured with hierarchical organs and the mystical body of Christ;
- the visible society and the spiritual community;
- the earthly Church and the Church endowed with heavenly riches" (*LG* 8). These dimensions together constitute "a complex reality which comes together from a human and a divine element" (*LG* 8) (*Catechism*, 771).

■ **B. How is the Church the sacrament of salvation?**
As sacrament, the Church is Christ's instrument. "She is taken up by him also as the instrument for the salvation of all," "the universal sacrament of salvation," by which Christ is "at once manifesting and actualizing the mystery of God's love for men" (*LG* 9 § 2, 48 § 2) (*Catechism*, 776).

■ **C. What are three ordinary meanings of the word Church?**
In Christian usage, the word "church" designates the liturgical assembly, but also the local community or the whole universal community of believers. These three meanings are inseparable (*Catechism*, 752).

1 Why is the church called the "People of God"?

God calls people to the church from all the peoples of the earth and forms them into "a chosen race, a royal priesthood, a holy nation" (1 Pt 2:9). Its members are initiated into the church through faith in Christ and baptism in his death and resurrection. Jesus is the head of God's people. The Holy Spirit dwells in the hearts of this people as in a temple. The law of this people is the commandment to love others as Christ loved us. This is the new law of the Holy Spirit. Its mission is to be the salt of the earth and the light of the world. Its destiny is the Kingdom of God begun on earth by God and completed by God at the end of time (cf. *Catechism, 782*).

2 Is there anything divine and mysterious about church community?

The church is a mystery, and as such it is imbued with God's hidden presence. Born of the Father's love, Christ's saving work and the outpouring of the Holy Spirit, the church reflects the mystery of God. The church, therefore, is the object of our faith.

3 How does Paul's image of the Body of Christ illustrate church community?

St. Paul uses the image of a body to teach church community because a body is not a superficial collection of parts. Rather, it is a unified and interrelated organism. By designating us as the Body of Christ, Paul takes us from the physical image to the essential spirituality of church community. As such, he said, we have unity and diversity through Jesus in the Spirit.

> **W**hatever light the church has flows from Jesus, the light of the world.

4 How did St. Paul describe the unity and diversity of the Body of Christ?

We are told to make "every effort to maintain the unity of the Spirit in the bond of peace. There is one body and one Spirit ... one Lord, one faith, one baptism, one God and Father of all. . ." (Eph 4:3-6).

The diversity of the community is underlined in his statement that "The body is one and has many members ... The eye cannot say to the hand, 'I have no need of you,' nor again the head to the feet, 'I have no need of you'... If one member suffers, all suffer together with it; if one member is honored, all rejoice together with it" (1 Cor 12:12,21,26).

5 What kind of values characterize church members?

The following traits are among the numerous values we expect to discover in the church's members: redemptive experience, love and affection, faith energy, common purpose, inspiring example, Catholic identity, sense of belonging, shared meaning and missionary dynamism. All these traits flow from our orientation to the Father through the Son in the Spirit.

6 How are Eucharist and church bonded together?

The church expresses and celebrates its communal identity in the celebration of the Eucharist. For early church members the words "Body of Christ" meant both the Eucharist and the church. Hence, Christ's body as Eucharist strengthened his body as church.

St. Paul asked, "The cup of blessing that we bless, is it not a sharing in the blood of Christ? The bread that we break, is it not a sharing in the body of Christ? Because there is one bread, we who are many, are one body, for we all partake of the one bread" (1 Cor 10:16,17).

7 Why should the church be a servant?

Jesus came to the world to serve, not to be served. What he did in one corner of the world at one place and time, the Body of Christ must do in all places at all times. Christ acted as servant-minister by his loving affection, compassion, healing and redemptive death and resurrection.

The church must take Jesus' example and continue to heal, serve and reconcile the people of the world by the graces of the Spirit. St. Paul teaches us that "All this is from God, who reconciled us to himself through Christ, and has given us the ministry of reconciliation" (2 Cor 5:18).

8 How is the church a sign of God's kingdom?

The law of the earthly kingdom is the love of power. The law of the kingdom of God is the power of love. It is the responsibility of the church community to give the world a glimpse of the Lord's kingdom. We must show others how to be a loving people, concerned with love, justice, peace and salvation—united by faith in Christ, empowered by the Holy Spirit, under the fatherhood of God.

9 Why is it important for us to see ourselves as a pilgrim church?

The church is not composed of members who are perfect. Rather, it is a gathering of sinful people striving for sanctity. As such, the church's members are pilgrims on a journey toward personal and communal holiness in the fullness of the Body of Christ.

The power of the risen Lord enables the church to have "strength to overcome patiently and lovingly the afflictions and hardships which assail her from within and without" (*Church*, 8). Christ's power enables God's people "to show forth in the world the mystery of the Lord in a faithful though shadowed way, until at the last it will be revealed in total splendor" *(Church, 8)*.

10 Is the church a missionary community?

"The pilgrim Church is missionary by her very nature" *(Decree on the Church's Missionary Activity*, 2). Every follower of Christ is called to witness and proclaim Jesus to others, especially to the unchurched. As St. Paul tells us, "And woe to me if I do not proclaim the gospel!" (1 Cor 9:16).

11 What are the "marks" of the church?

In the Creed of Nicea we confess that the church is one, holy, catholic and apostolic. These are the four marks or signs of church identity.

12 How are the marks of the church defined?

One: This refers to the unity of Catholics, who are bonded together by Christ in his Spirit with shared beliefs and values. "The highest exemplar and source of this mystery is the unity, in the Trinity of Persons, of one God, the Father and the Son in the Holy Spirit" (*Catechism*, 813). This unity also is a goal yet to be achieved as we strive to become a people of one mind and heart in God. Moreover, the church seeks the goal, in ecumenism, of unity with all Christian churches.

Holy: The Holy Spirit is the holiness of the church. Our union with the Holy Spirit engenders holiness in each of us, seen most dramatically in saints and mystics. It also is evidenced in the striving of ordinary people to live loving, holy and worthwhile lives.

> *We have unity and diversity through Jesus in the spirit.*

Catholic: "The Church is Catholic because Christ is present in her. 'Where there is Christ Jesus, there is the Catholic Church'" (*Catechism*, 830). The word catholic means universal. Our church has heard Christ's call to bring the good news of salvation to all nations and continues to fulfill this mission.

Apostolic: Our church was founded on the apostles, the witnesses chosen and sent by Christ himself. It is apostolic also because it guards and transmits the teaching of the apostles under the guidance of the Spirit. Thirdly, the church is apostolic since it is taught, sanctified and guided by their successors, the popes and bishops, and the priests who assist them (cf. *Catechism*, 857).

13 What is the diversity of church within the Catholic communion?

Catholicism is made up of the church of the West (Latin church) and the churches of the East, which have their origins in the apostolic churches of Jerusalem, Antioch, Alexandria and Constantinople. Through the centuries, the Eastern and Western churches have developed traditions, theologies, liturgies and forms of spirituality of their own.

The Eastern church is organized according to major traditions: Byzantine, Antiochene, Chaldean, Armenian and Alexandrian. Pope John Paul II speaks of this union of the churches of East and West as "one Church breathing with two lungs."

14 Why do we speak of the church as an institution?

All communities require organizational procedures, such as rules of order, officers and distribution of responsibilities. This is no less true of our church. "For the nurturing and constant growth of the People of God, Christ the Lord instituted in His Church a variety of ministries, which work for the good of the whole body" (*Church*, 18).

15   How did Jesus organize his church?

In choosing his twelve apostles, with Peter as the head, Jesus created the basic element in any organization, that of hierarchical leadership. He mandated them to continue his prophetic, priestly and kingly ministry as follows:

Prophetic: "Whoever welcomes you welcomes me ... Go therefore and make disciples of all nations ... teaching them to obey everything that I have commanded you" (Mt 10:40; 28:19-20).
Priestly: They were to be the leaders in worship. Regarding the Eucharistic, sacrificial meal, Jesus told them, "Do this in remembrance of me"

> *It is the responsibility of the church community to give the world a glimpse of the Lord's kingdom.*

(Lk 22:19). They also were to be ministers of reconciliation. This is witnessed by Christ's command, "As the Father has sent me, so I send you ... Receive the Holy Spirit. If you forgive the sins of any, they are forgiven them" (Jn 20:21-23).
Kingly: The apostles taught and acted with authority. At the first Apostolic Council in Jerusalem, they issued a decree with these words:

"It has seemed good to the Holy Spirit and to us" (Acts 15:28; cf. Gal 1:6-9).

These ministries were passed on to the popes and bishops as successors of Peter and the apostles. "The apostles took care to appoint successors in this hierarchically structured society" (*Church*, 20).

16   What role did Christ choose for St. Peter ?

Jesus chose Peter to be the leader of the apostles and the church, naming him rock of the church at Caesarea Philippi (Mt 16:18) and shepherd of the church at the Galilean lakeshore (Jn 21:15-17).

17   What is the relationship of bishops and pope?

Christ appointed the Twelve after the manner "of a college or a fixed group, over which He placed Peter, chosen from among them" (*Church*, 19). Just as "by the Lord's will, St. Peter and the other apostles constituted one apostolic college, so in a similar way the Roman Pontiff as the successor of Peter, and the bishops as the successors of the apostles are joined together" (*Church*, 22).

18   Who is the pope?

The word pope means father. The pope is the vicar of Christ, Bishop of Rome, successor of St. Peter and worldwide leader of the Catholic Church.

THE CELEBRATION OF THE CHRISTIAN MYSTERIES

The creeds of the church outline the history and the mystery of salvation. The sacraments of the church continue God's work of salvation in our own day. In each sacramental celebration we go to the Father, through Jesus in the Spirit. The building blocks of the church's liturgical life are: (1) the Body of Christ at worship; (2) the paschal mystery; (3) the celebration of the Christian mysteries.

Our life of worship is always a communal event because it is the Body of Christ at prayer. Ideally, therefore, each liturgical event should be with the Christian assembly. Yet even when an individual prays the Liturgy of the Hours alone, this prayer—because it is the prayer of the Body of Christ—graces the whole church.

Secondly, celebrations of sacraments are always paschal mystery events. They are mysteries because of the divine action of Father, Son and Spirit working through the bishop, priest, deacon and assembly. They are paschal because they always communicate the dying and rising of Jesus—a death to sin and life unto God. Hence we should be dying to sin and rising to divine life in each celebration.

Thirdly, we speak of sacramental events as celebrations because they are saving events in which the whole communion of saints is involved. Liturgies on earth are connected to the heavenly liturgy of Mary, the angels and the saints united with Jesus Christ, leading all to the Father in the Spirit (cf. *Catechism*, 1090). We celebrate divine salvation with joy and express it on earth through our sacraments in an assembly of loving, believing and hope-filled people.

The Celebration of the Christian Mysteries

■ **A. What is a sacrament?**

The sacraments are efficacious signs of grace, instituted by Christ and entrusted to the Church, by which divine life is dispensed to us. The visible rites by which the sacraments are celebrated signify and make present the graces proper to each sacrament. They bear fruit in those who receive them with the required dispositions (*Catechism*, 1131).

■ **B. How is the Holy Spirit connected to liturgy?**

In the liturgy the Holy Spirit is teacher of the faith of the People of God and artisan of "God's masterpieces," the sacraments of the New Covenant. The desire and work of the Spirit in the heart of the Church is that we may live from the life of the risen Christ. When the Spirit encounters in us the response of faith which he has aroused in us, he brings about genuine cooperation. Through it, the liturgy becomes the common work of the Holy Spirit and the Church (*Catechism*, 1091).

■ **C. What is Christ's action in the sacraments?**

Celebrated worthily in faith, the sacraments confer the grace that they signify. They are *efficacious* because in them Christ himself is at work: it is he who baptizes, he who acts in his sacraments in order to communicate the grace that each sacrament signifies. The Father always hears the prayer of his Son's Church which, in the epiclesis of each sacrament, expresses her faith in the power of the Spirit. As fire transforms into itself everything it touches, so the Holy Spirit transforms into the divine life whatever is subjected to his power (*Catechism*, 1127).

1 What are the seven sacraments of the church?

The seven sacraments are baptism, confirmation, Eucharist, reconciliation, anointing of the sick, holy orders and matrimony.

2 What is the meaning of each of the seven sacraments?

The meaning of each sacrament is as follows:

Baptism: This sacrament initiates us into the Christian life and the church. Baptism marks us as one who has been saved by Jesus Christ and sanctified with the Spirit of God. "Do you not know that all of us who have been baptized into Christ Jesus were baptized into his death? ... we have been buried with him by baptism into death, so that, just as Christ was raised from the dead by the glory of the Father, so we too might walk in newness of life" (Rom 6:3,4).

Through the sign of the baptismal waters, the recipient experiences death to all sin, original and actual, and new life in Christ.

> *The Eucharist makes present the sacrificial death and glorious resurrection of Christ for our salvation.*

Confirmation: This sacrament of initiation seals us with the Holy Spirit. Confirmation empowers us to serve the Kingdom of God boldly, for we are told, "When Paul had laid his hands on them, the Holy Spirit came upon them, and they spoke in tongues and prophesied ..." Thus did the word of the Lord continue to spread with influence and power (Acts 19:6,20).

Therefore, through the signs of laying on of hands and sealing with oil in confirmation, the bishop or his priest-delegate "passes on" the gifts received in the Spirit.

Eucharist: This sacrament completes our initiation into the church. "For the most blessed Eucharist contains the Church's entire spiritual wealth, that is, Christ Himself, our Passover and the living bread" (*Decree on the Ministry and Life of Priests,* 5).

The Eucharist makes present the sacrificial death and glorious resurrection of Christ for our salvation. The Eucharist is also Communion, a sacrificial meal, in which we share the divine life promised to us. By the power of the Spirit and the action of the priest, the bread and wine are transformed into the body and blood of Jesus. Jesus is truly present in the blessed sacrament.

Reconciliation: Also called penance or confession, the sacrament of reconciliation is the formal celebration of a sinner's repentance for sins, God's forgiveness through the absolution of the priest and the penitent's promise of satisfaction and amendment of life. Scripture tells us that Jesus said, "Your sins are forgiven ... Your faith has saved you; go in peace" (Lk 7:48,50).

Jesus proclaimed the good news of forgiveness for sins. In the sacrament of reconciliation we experience that forgiveness and are reconciled once again with God, with church and with ourselves.

Anointing of the Sick: This sacrament (also one of reconciliation), which is the liturgical prayer for seriously ill church members, was formerly called extreme unction. "Are any among you sick? They should call for the elders of the church ... The prayer of faith will save the sick, and the Lord will raise them up; and anyone who has committed sins will be forgiven" (James 5:14,15).

The signs of holy oil and laying on of hands used in administering this sacrament express our faith in God's power over sickness and the meaning of suffering in the life of the community.

Holy Orders: Called by God and the bishops of the church, certain men are chosen and anointed in this sacrament to serve the church as deacons, priests and bishops. Holy orders is a sacrament of service. Bishops, priests and deacons are called to serve the sanctification needs of the laity, who are members of the common priesthood acquired in their baptism.

Marriage: Marriage, a sacrament of service, is the rite by which the matrimonial bond becomes a sign of God's love and union with his people. "Husbands, love your wives, just as Christ loved the church" (Eph 5:25).

Through this sacrament, the spouses see a sign of the depth and permanence of God's love and pledge a permanent union with each other. In addition, the spouses vow to love each other until death and declare their intention to have children and raise, nurture and educate them in the Christian faith.

3 What connections are there among the sacraments?

The sacraments of baptism, confirmation and Eucharist are called the sacraments of initiation because they are the steps toward full participation in the paschal mystery of Christ and membership in the church.

> *Each sacramental event offers us an encounter with Jesus.*

The sacrament of reconciliation (confession) and the sacrament of anointing are called sacraments of healing, inasmuch as they involve healing of the person, soul, mind and body.

The sacraments of service are holy orders and matrimony, directed at service to the church and the world.

4 What does the church teach about the sacraments?

The church teaches that sacraments are the saving acts of Jesus Christ, designed to assist church members on their faith journey to eternal life. Each sacramental event offers us an encounter with Jesus leading us to the Father in the Spirit, in the context of the community of believers. In that experience of faith and grace, we can share a deeper, loving union with the Lord and church community members.

5 Who celebrates a sacrament?

"The liturgy is the work of the whole Christ, head and body. Our high priest celebrates it unceasingly in the heavenly liturgy, with the holy Mother of God, the apostles, all the saints, and the multitude of those who have already entered the kingdom. In a liturgical celebration, the whole assembly is *leitourgos*, each member according to his own function. The baptismal priesthood is that of the whole Body of Christ. But some of the faithful are ordained through the sacrament of Holy Orders to represent Christ as head of the Body" (*Catechism*, 1187-88).

6 Why are just these seven events called sacraments?

"As she has done for the canon of Sacred Scripture and for the doctrine of the faith, the Church, by the power of the Spirit who guides her 'into all truth,' has gradually recognized this treasure received from Christ and, as the faithful steward of God's mysteries, has determined its 'dispensation.' Thus the Church has discerned over the centuries that among liturgical celebrations there are seven that are, in the strict sense of the term, sacraments instituted by the Lord" (*Catechism*, 1117).

7 What part should sacraments play in our overall religious life?

Sacraments are gifts made available to us, which we should treasure and use well. Some sacraments become high points in personal and community faith life. Such is the usual experience at baptisms and confirmations, where the community is conscious of sharing its faith. Here, the recipient is the *center* of real love.

Holy orders and marriage should be occasions where people are clear about the Lord's place in their lives and the commitment they are about to make. The anointing of the sick helps bring spiritual and physical renewal to those who are ill.

Eucharist and reconciliation are the sacraments we receive most often. They should be a mainstay of support and strength in our battle against evil. We do, however, run the risk of taking them for granted or celebrating them thoughtlessly. These sacraments should not be seen as less valuable because of their availability.

8 May Protestants receive the sacraments in the Catholic Church?

Sacraments are experiences that both form and express the *unity* of our church. For that reason they may only be received by Catholics. That is why people who are not Catholic, even those who are baptized in another Christian religion, are not usually invited to receive the sacraments. Unfortunately, this is one of the most painful evidences of our lack of unity as Christians and should serve as an impetus to work for *real unity* of faith.

9 Should we feel good every time we receive a sacrament?

Feelings of closeness to the Lord are valuable. We should see such emotions as *gifts* from God and thank him when we do experience these feelings. However, feelings are not primary. More essential are the proper intentions of our minds and the orientation of our wills toward God. It is important that we receive sacraments to worship God, praise him for his salvation and to deepen the Lord's presence in our lives.

> *Your sins are forgiven ... Your faith has saved you; go in peace.*

10 What is the relationship of personal prayer to the sacraments?

Times of personal prayer, Scripture reading and experiences of God's presence in our daily lives are essential parts of our religious lives. Once we have the foundation of a deep, spiritual relationship, we should nourish it and express it in a multitude of ways. In addition, we can become more attentive to the Lord's presence when we receive the sacraments.

11 What are *sacramentals?*

Sacramentals are reminders of God's presence in our lives. Pictures, statues and medals of Jesus and the saints are sacramentals used by Catholics to call us to prayer.

12 What is the value of the Liturgy of the Hours?

"The faithful who celebrate the Liturgy of the Hours are united to Christ our high priest, by the prayer of the Psalms, meditation on the Word of God, and canticles and blessings, in order to be joined with his unceasing and universal prayer that gives glory to the Father and implores the gift of the Holy Spirit on the whole world" (*Catechism*, 1196).

The Liturgy of the Hours prolongs the celebration of the Eucharist, flowing from the altar and flowing back to the altar. This prayer of the church, returning again and again to God at set hours of the day and night, is a fulfillment of Scripture's command, "Pray without ceasing" (1 Thess 5:17).

THE SACRAMENTS OF INITIATION

How do we celebrate sacraments?

First, with signs and symbols. God teaches us through human nature, culture and the work of creation, and the events of the Old Testament covenant. Jesus often used created symbols and gestures to reveal the mysteries of the Kingdom of God. He gave new meaning to the symbols of the covenant because he is the ultimate meaning of these signs. Since Pentecost, the Spirit accomplishes our sanctification through the sacramental signs of the church.

Second, with words and actions. At liturgy we encounter Father, Son and Spirit in a dialogue of words and deeds of faith. The ceremonies that surround the proclamation of the word (honoring the lectionary with processions, candles and incense) and the homily, accompanied by acclamations, psalms, litanies and professions of faith, nourish faith and make present the wonders proclaimed.

Third, with singing and music. "How I wept, deeply moved by your hymns, songs and the voices that echoed through your Church! What emotions I experienced in them! Those sounds flowed into my ears, distilling the truth in my heart. A feeling of devotion surged within me, and tears streamed down my face—tears that did me good" (Augustine, *Commentary on Psalm 72*).

Fourth, in liturgical time. Someone has said, "I take off my watch when Mass starts. I leave standard time behind and enter heaven's time." Sunday is the Lord's Day, the day for celebrating the Eucharist, because Jesus rose from the dead on Sunday. It is a Christian family day and a day to rest from work. It is the heart of the week. In liturgical seasons from Advent to Pentecost, the church unfolds the whole mystery of Christ and our expectation for His coming.

The Sacraments of Initiation

■ **A. Why do we speak of sacraments of initiation?**
The sacraments of Christian initiation—Baptism, Confirmation, and the Eucharist—lay the *foundations* of every Christian life. "The sharing in the divine nature given to men through the grace of Christ bears a certain likeness to the origin, development, and nourishing of natural life. The faithful are born anew by Baptism, strengthened by the sacrament of Confirmation, and receive in the Eucharist the food of eternal life. By means of these sacraments of Christian initiation, they thus receive in increasing measure the treasures of the divine life and advance toward the perfection of charity" (Paul VI, *Participants in the Divine Nature*, AAS, 63) (*Catechism*, 1212).

■ **B. What is the significance of baptism?**
Holy Baptism is the basis of the whole Christian life, the gateway to life in the Spirit (*vitae spiritualis ianua*), and the door which gives access to the other sacraments. Through Baptism we are freed from sin and reborn as sons of God; we become members of Christ, are incorporated into the Church and made sharers in her mission: "Baptism is the sacrament of regeneration through water in the word" (*Roman Catechism II*, 2,5) (*Catechism*, 1213).

■ **C. What does confirmation do for us?**
Confirmation perfects Baptismal grace; it is the sacrament which gives the Holy Spirit in order to root us more deeply in the divine filiation, incorporate us more firmly into Christ, strengthen our bond with the Church, associate us more closely with her mission, and help us bear witness to the Christian faith in words accompanied by deeds (*Catechism*, 1316).

1 What helps us receive a sacrament more effectively?

A sacrament is a visible efficacious sign, or ritual experience, in which we encounter Christ's saving love in the context of church. In this event, our capacity to be open to Christ's actions depends upon the depth of our faith disposition, which is helped by the Holy Spirit. Therefore, the sacramental event is like a dialogue or encounter between Christ and ourselves. We should pray to the Spirit for all the graces we need to be ready for the sacrament.

2 What is the role of the assembly in sacraments?

We do not engage in sacramental celebrations only as individuals. Rather, we share these experiences as members of the worshiping assembly, the Body of Christ. The faith witness of other members of the assembly helps our own. We are saved within the context of community.

3 What are the sacraments of initiation?

Baptism, confirmation and the Eucharist are the sacraments of initiation. Through the rites of initiation, a person is introduced to full communion with the holy Trinity, the communion of saints and the Body of Christ on earth.

4 What is baptism?

Baptism is the sacrament of faith by which, through the Spirit's power, men and women accept Christ's call to salvation and the Kingdom of God. Moreover, the newly baptized are incorporated into Christ and the church. They obtain forgiveness of all their sins, both original and actual, and become a "new creation" through water and the Holy Spirit.

We are saved within the context of community.

5 Why is water used in the baptismal rite?

Baptism is a term that refers to a cleansing with water. In the sacrament of baptism, men and women are spiritually cleansed with water by the power of the Spirit in Jesus. The Lord gave himself up for the church "to make her holy by cleansing her with the washing of water" (Eph 5:26).

The church's prayers for the blessing of the water announce it to be the water of cleansing rebirth. Thus, in baptism we are born again. As Paul wrote to Titus, "He saved us ... through the water of rebirth and renewal by the Holy Spirit" (Ti 3:5).

6 Why is the blessed Trinity invoked over those to be baptized?

Through invocation of the holy Trinity at baptism, we are consecrated to God and brought into loving union with the Father, Son and Spirit. By our faith, we profess our belief and trust in the saving love of the Trinity.

7 How does faith play a role in the sacrament of baptism?

Baptism is a sacrament of our faith in Christ. During baptism we make our faith decision to accept Christ's salvation and to become a member of the church. The link between faith and baptism is shown in the New Testament. "For in Christ Jesus you are all children of God through faith. As many of you as were baptized into Christ have clothed yourselves with Christ" (Gal 3:26-27).

8 What are the major stages in the Rite of Christian Initiation of Adults (Latin Rite)?

The major stages of the Rite of Christian Initiation of Adults are:

Evangelization: Adults hear the Gospel of Jesus, and the Holy Spirit opens their hearts to his message. Voluntarily and consciously they seek God and begin a journey in faith and further conversion. At this time, they seek admittance to the church.

Catechumenate: The adults become catechumens or candidates for the sacrament of initiation. This period is marked by a series of liturgical rites, training in prayer, spiritual and moral living and instruction in the fundamentals of Christian life and spiritual teaching.

Illumination: The church formally "elects" them for full membership. Usually occurring during Lent, this phase gives the elect an opportunity to seek purification as they enter into more profound spiritual preparation for the sacraments. Throughout these stages the candidates are brought in touch with the church community to experience their support and to begin a gradual identification with the People of God.

This phase normally concludes at the Easter Vigil, when catechumens are baptized, confirmed and celebrate their first Eucharist.

Mystagogia: During the Easter season the newborn members of the church reflect upon and assimilate the meaning of the sacraments and the church. They continue to meditate on Scripture and to share the Eucharist and church life. They also are urged to do works of love, justice and mercy that are the behavioral signs of the kingdom.

> **A**s many of you as were baptized into Christ have clothed yourselves with Christ.

9 What are the qualities one should have to serve as a godparent?

According to ancient church tradition, persons serving as godparents should help prepare the one to be baptized. After the person has received the sacrament, the godparent should assist the person in maintaining a good Christian life.

Godparents should be capable of such responsibility, should have themselves received the sacraments of initiation and should be members in good standing of the Catholic Church.

10 At what age has the church traditionally baptized a person?

From the earliest days of Christianity the church has baptized infants as well as adults. Jesus said that "... no one can enter the kingdom of God without being born of water and Spirit" (Jn 3:5).

The church calls on the parents and godparents of the infants to proclaim their faith on behalf of the children. Subsequently, these adults have the responsibility to help form these children in the beliefs, attitudes and practices of the Catholic Church.

11 What is expected of the parents of infants being baptized?

Parents should prepare for the baptism of their infant with faith, prayer and adequate understanding of the sacrament. This includes taking instructions and visits with a priest and lay parish members who can help the parents with pastoral advice and prayer. Parents should be present at the baptismal celebration and assume the parts assigned to them.

Lastly, the church expects the parents to take responsibility to help their children come to know and love God, to receive confirmation and to share in the Eucharistic celebrations.

12 What is baptism of desire?

There are millions of people in the world who have not had an opportunity to hear the Gospel. Traditional Catholic teaching described actions by people of good will as baptism of desire.

We are told that people also can attain to everlasting salvation who "... through no fault of their own do not know the gospel of Christ or His Church, yet sincerely seek God and, moved by grace, strive by their deeds to do His will as it is known to them through the dictates of conscience" (*Church*, 16).

13 What place does confirmation have in the progress of the sacraments of initiation?

Pope Paul VI described the flow of the sacraments of initiation in this manner: "The faithful are born anew by baptism, strengthened by the sacrament of confirmation and finally sustained by the food of eternal life in the eucharist."

Tertullian, an early father of the church, situates confirmation as "The body is washed that the soul may be cleansed. The body is anointed and overshadowed by the laying on of hands that the soul may be enlightened by the Holy Spirit. The body is fed by the Body of Christ that the soul be nourished by God."

14   What New Testament experiences underline the meaning of confirmation?

Scripture associates confirmation with the gift of the Holy Spirit and the laying on of hands. On Pentecost the apostles received the Holy Spirit whom Jesus promised to send. "If I do not go away, the Advocate will not come to you; but if I go, I will send him to you" (Jn 16:7). The apostles also received the power of conferring the Holy Spirit after baptism.

> *Confirmation brings an increase and deepening of baptismal grace.*

"Simon saw that the Spirit was given through the laying on of the apostles' hands ..." (Acts 8:18). Later, "When Paul had laid his hands on them, the Holy Spirit came upon them..." (Acts 19:6).

15   What is confirmation?

"Confirmation brings an increase and deepening of baptismal grace:
— it roots us more deeply in the divine filiation which makes us cry, 'Abba! Father!';
— it unites us more firmly to Christ;
— it increases the gifts of the Holy Spirit in us;
— it renders our bond with the Church more perfect;
— it gives us a special strength of the Holy Spirit to spread and defend the faith by word and action as true witnesses of Christ, to confess the name of Christ boldly, and never to be ashamed of the Cross" (*Catechism*, 1303).

16   What are the basic elements of confirmation?

Confirmation is made up of the post-baptismal ceremonies of anointing with oil, the laying on of hands and the words, "Be sealed with the gift of the Holy Spirit."

17   What is the primary significance of anointing the receiver with oil at confirmation?

The oil used during confirmation is known as chrism, or "anointing oil." Historically, rubbing oil was put on athletes' muscles to increase strength. Similarly, the use of oil of chrism is meant to *tone up* the attitudes, spirit and resolve of those receiving confirmation. This helps them live out Christian commitment by the power of the Spirit.

The consecrated chrism symbolizes the Holy Spirit. It is an outward symbol of the invisible Spirit who is the real "oil power" of our souls.

THE BREAD OF LIFE

The *Catechism* illustrates the richness of the meaning of Eucharist by listing nine ways in which it can be described.

It is called Eucharist because it is an act of thanksgiving to God.

It is known as the Lord's Supper because it re-enacts the last supper the Lord ate on the eve of his passion.

Early Christians called it the Breaking of the Bread because Jesus used this rite, proper to Jewish meals, when as Master of the Table he blessed and distributed bread.

We call it the Eucharistic assembly because it is celebrated in the assembly of believers, the visible expression of church.

It is also called the memorial of the Lord's passion and resurrection.

The church calls it the Holy Sacrifice of the Mass because it makes present the one sacrifice of Christ the savior and includes the church's own offering.

The church in the East calls it the Holy and Divine Liturgy because the church's whole liturgy finds its center and most intense expression in its celebration.

It is called Communion because by this sacrament we are united to Christ who enables us to share in his body and form a single body.

In the Latin Church it is called the Holy Mass because the liturgy concludes with words that send forth the faithful on mission to do God's will in their lives (cf.

Catechism, 1328-1332). All these terms are essentially related to one another. Together they give us a comprehensive view of Eucharist.

The Bread of Life

■ **A. How central is the mystery of the Eucharist?**
The Eucharist is "the source and summit of the Christian life." "The other sacraments, and indeed all ecclesiastical ministries and works of the apostolate, are bound up with the Eucharist and are oriented toward it. For in the blessed Eucharist is contained the whole spiritual good of the Church, namely Christ himself, our Pasch" (*Priests*, 5) (*Catechism,* 1324).

■ **B. How does the altar signify the Eucharist as Christ's sacrifice on the cross and the sacred banquet of communion?**
The altar, around which the Church is gathered in the celebration of the Eucharist, represents the two aspects of the same mystery: the altar of the sacrifice and the table of the Lord. This is all the more so since the Christian altar is the symbol of Christ himself, present in the midst of the assembly of his faithful, both as the victim offered for our reconciliation and as food from heaven who is giving himself to us... "The altar represents the body [of Christ] and the Body of Christ is on the altar" (Ambrose, *Sacraments*, 4,2) (*Catechism*, 1383).

■ **C. What are the essential signs of the Eucharist?**
The essential signs of the Eucharistic sacrament are wheat bread and grape wine, on which the blessing of the Holy Spirit is invoked and the priest pronounces the words of consecration spoken by Jesus during the Last Supper: "This is my body which will be given up for you ... This is the cup of my blood ..." (*Catechism*, 1412).

1 What is the significance of the Passover meal?

The Passover meal is a festive remembrance of the deliverance of the Israelites from bondage in Egypt. It also celebrates God's continuous care for his people throughout history and illustrates a major event in his plan for our salvation.

2 What is the symbolism of the food served during the Passover meal?

The herbs and sauce are the foods of slavery. The bitter herbs recall the oppressive slavery in Egypt. The clay-colored sauce evokes the memory of the tedious hours of brickmaking in the heat of the Egyptian sun. The unleavened bread and the lamb are the foods of freedom. The unleavened bread teaches the haste with which the Jews fled Egypt. There was no time to leaven dough for the next day's supply.

The lamb that is eaten is a special Paschal lamb, the blood of which is reminiscent of that which marked their ancestors' door posts as a sign for the avenging angel to "pass over" them in the tenth plague.

Those attending the meal drink four cups of red wine, symbolizing the saving blood of the lamb and heart warming fellowship of the people at the feast.

3 What are the major events of Christ's Passover meal?

Following is one possible construction of the events of the Last Supper.

At the beginning of the meal Jesus washed the apostles' feet, symbolizing his personal humility which foreshadowed his passion. This act of purification is similar to the penance service that now begins each eucharistic celebration.

Next came the first cup of wine, accompanied by a meal prayer and the memory of the first passover. Jesus used this part of the meal to teach his followers, to pray with them and to sing the Great Hallel Psalm 113 with them (cf. Jn 14:17).

Jesus then broke the bread. As he did so, Jesus spoke his startling new words: "This is my body, which is given for you. Do this in remembrance of me" (Lk 22:19; cf. Jn 6). Jesus distributed the bread that had become his body.

Jesus then served the Passover lamb, the bitter herbs and the sauce. The sacrificial lamb sym-

bolized the sacrifice of Jesus the Lamb of God. They drank the second cup of wine.

After the meal Jesus took the third cup of wine and said, "This is my blood of the covenant, which is poured out for many" (Mk 14:24). His new covenant echoed the prophet Jeremiah's words, when he said, "I will make a new covenant with the house of Israel ..." (Jer 31:31). He distributed the wine that had become his blood.

The meal ended with the fourth cup of wine. Drinking it, they sang, "I will lift up the cup of salvation ... I shall not die, but I shall live" (Ps 116:13; 118:17).

4 How does Christ's Passover meal relate to our understanding of the Eucharist?

Jesus identified the bread and wine with his own body and blood, foreseeing his own sacrificial death. As the unleavened bread was broken so is his body broken, and as the wine is poured so is his blood shed.

Just as the lamb was offered up in prayer and sacrifice at the temple, so would Jesus, the Lamb of God, be sacrificed for the salvation of sinners and the reconciliation of all men and women with God.

> *The word Eucharist comes from the Greek word for thanksgiving.*

5 What is the meaning of the word *Eucharist*?

The word *Eucharist* comes from the Greek word for *thanksgiving*. It is used because Jesus gave thanks at the Last Supper and associates us with him in perfect thanksgiving and praise each time the Mass is offered (Lk 22:19; Mt 26:27).

6 What does it mean for us to be involved in the Eucharist?

When Jesus distributed the bread and wine to his apostles, he invited them to share his sacrifice and the power of his atoning death. When we participate in the eucharistic celebration, we partake of the body and the blood of Jesus and share in his

> *When we participate in the eucharistic celebration, we partake of the body and the blood of Jesus and share in his sacrifice.*

sacrifice. We implicitly promise to be "as bread that is broken," and commit ourselves to work for the kingdom of love, justice and mercy.

7 What is the meaning of Christ's words, "Do this as a remembrance of me"?

The apostles were asked to "remember" Jesus' celebration on several levels. He asked that they repeat the Last Supper event in the "breaking of the bread," or eucharistic celebration. Also, they were to make present the saving work of Jesus. "The cup of blessing that we bless, is it not a sharing in the blood of Christ? The bread that we break, is it not a sharing in the body of Christ?" (1 Cor 10:16). The third level is the final fulfillment of Jesus' kingdom at the end of time. "For as often as you eat this bread and drink the cup, you proclaim the Lord's death until he comes" (1 Cor 11:26).

Thus, our eucharistic memory works on three levels: we recall the past events of the Last Supper and the salvation events that followed it; we experience the immediate presence of those events in terms of the active presence of Jesus along with his saving sacrifice, grace, love and power; and we anticipate the fulfillment of Christ's work as his kingdom continues to come into being.

8 How did the settings for Eucharist evolve?

From the New Testament days and through almost 300 years of the church's early history, the Eucharist was celebrated in a member's home. Gradually, the celebration of the Eucharist was transferred to a church. Here an altar replaced the family table, and formalities such as elaborate ceremonies, processions, incense and large crowds soon replaced the informal environment of the home.

9 What are the major parts of the eucharistic celebration?

The eucharistic liturgy is composed of the Liturgy of the Word and the Liturgy of the Eucharist. They are described as:

Liturgy of the Word: This part of the celebration includes psalms, hymns, Bible readings and a homily. Here, Christ comes to us as the living Word and calls us to a deeper love and union with him and with each other. He asks us to say *yes* to him and to the salvation he offers us. In addition, he invites us to identify with his sacrificial love and to commit ourselves to advancing the Kingdom of God.

Liturgy of the Eucharist: Its components are the preparation of the gifts, the Eucharistic Prayer (including the words of invocation of the Spirit and those of the institution from the Last Supper), the Communion and the concluding prayer. Jesus enters our midst *sacramentally* in his body and blood. As such, he communicates his healing, loving and reconciling grace and power. To the extent that we believe, Jesus fills our hearts with his richest spiritual gifts.

10 How is the Eucharist a "sacrifice"?

The Eucharist is a sacrifice of praise, thanksgiving, atonement and expiation for the living and the dead. Just as Christ acted as priest and victim at Calvary, so he does at the Eucharist but in an unbloody manner. The sacrifice of Calvary and that of the Eucharist are one and the same.

11 Why is adoration of the Real Presence important?

The eucharistic presence of Christ begins at the moment of the consecration and endures as long as the eucharistic elements are present ... "The Church and the world have a great need for eucharistic worship. Jesus awaits us in this sacrament of love. Let us not refuse time to go meet him in adoration, in contemplation full of faith and open to making amends for the serious offenses and crimes of the world. May our adoration never cease" (Pope John Paul II, *Lord's Supper*, 3).

12 Is Christ fully present in both the consecrated bread and the wine?

Some teachers of theology during the Middle Ages and the Reformation argued that it was necessary to receive communion under both consecrated forms, the bread and the wine. They said that by doing otherwise one does not fully encounter Christ.

The church's response was that Jesus is *fully present* under both forms and to commune with one species is sufficient. But taking communion under both species is becoming more common as an accepted practice in the Latin Rite church.

13 What is the role of the priest at Eucharist?

At Eucharist, priests act in the person of Christ, proclaim his mystery and unite the prayers of the faithful with the sacrifice of Jesus. Until the Lord's return, priests make present again the one sacrifice of the cross, the unique self offering of Christ, to the Father. The priest represents Christ as head of the church and acts on behalf of the assembly when offering the eucharistic sacrifice.

14 What is the role of the faithful while assembled at Mass?

"The Church, therefore, earnestly desires that Christ's faithful, when present at this mystery of faith, should not be there as strangers or silent spectators ... through a proper appreciation of the rites and prayers they should participate knowingly, devoutly, and actively. They should be instructed by God's word and be refreshed at the table of the Lord's body; ... by offering the Immaculate Victim, not only through the hands of the priest, but also with him, they should learn to offer themselves too" (*Liturgy*, 48).

15 What is the connection between the Eucharist and our daily lives?

The Eucharist makes present Christ's plan of salvation and his desire to establish a kingdom of love, justice and mercy here on earth. In the Eucharist we are liberated from sin. We gain the motivational power to share the Gospel with others in our homes, neighborhoods and throughout the world. We do this as individuals and as members of a church community.

In particular, our eucharistic vocation summons us to seek justice and peace everywhere. The Bread of Life is meant to be bread for the poor, the oppressed and those who are denied religious freedom.

16 What preparations are made for the first reception of the sacrament of Eucharist?

Holy Communion is the third of the three sacraments of initiation for adults. The first two are baptism and confirmation. Through the Rite of Christian Initiation of Adults, the candidate is prepared for all three sacraments.

Parents, catechists and parish pastors determine when children are ready to receive their First Communion. Parents have a special responsibility to help their children appreciate the reality and meaning of the Eucharist and call them to faith, reverence and love according to their abilities.

17 What is the Communion fast?

Fasting before receiving Holy Communion helps us to prepare for being open to Christ's love. It is observed one hour before receiving communion, at which time church members abstain from solid foods and beverages. Water and medicine may be taken at any time.

18 What is a Catholic's "Easter Duty"?

All Catholics are expected to go to Holy Communion once a year—if possible, during the Easter season, spanning the time from Easter Sunday to Trinity Sunday (cf. *Catechism*, 1389). Normally, Catholics should receive communion at every opportunity, since that is the most meaningful way to complete participation in the Eucharist.

FORGIVE ME, FATHER

Jesus is the doctor of our souls and bodies. He forgave the sins of the paralytic and also restored his bodily health. Jesus gave the church the Holy Spirit, by whose power this healing ministry could continue. Such is the purpose of the sacraments of healing—reconciliation and anointing of the sick.

The sacrament of reconciliation is related to conversion from sin. This is the first step we all take on our journey to the Father. This sacrament is called the sacrament of conversion because it accomplishes this step sacramentally.

We also speak of the sacrament of penance, because it includes turning from sin and doing penance for our sins.

It is also called the sacrament of confession, since telling our sins to a priest is an essential part of the sacrament.

It is referred to as the sacrament of forgiveness since by the priest's sacramental absolution the penitent receives pardon and peace from God.

It is known as the sacrament of reconciliation because it reconciles us to God and to the church and prepares us to respond to God's call to be reconciled to our brothers and sisters.

Forgive Me, Father

■ A. Why do we need a sacrament of reconciliation after baptism?

The new life received in Christian initiation has not abolished the frailty and weakness of human nature, nor the inclination to sin that tradition calls *concupiscence,* which remains in the baptized such that with the help of the grace of Christ they may prove themselves in the struggle of Christian life (*Catechism,* 1426). The apostle John also says: "If we say we have no sin, we deceive ourselves, and the truth is not in us" (1 *Jn* 1:8). And the Lord himself taught us to pray: "Forgive us our trespass-es," linking our forgiveness of one another's offenses to the forgiveness of our sins that God will grant us (*Catechism,* 1425).

■ B. How do we practice daily conversion of heart?

Conversion is accomplished in daily life by gestures of reconciliation, concern for the poor, the exercise and *Action* defense of justice and right, by the admission of faults to one's brethren, fraternal correction, revision of life, examination of conscience, spiritual direction, acceptance of suffering, endurance of persecution for the sake of righteousness. Taking up one's cross each day and following Jesus is the surest way of penance (*Catechism,* 1435).

■ C. Why did Jesus give us the sacrament of reconciliation?

Christ instituted the sacrament of Penance for all sinful members of his Church: above all for those who, since Baptism, have fallen into grave sin, and have thus lost their baptismal grace and wounded ecclesial communion. It is to them that the sacrament of Penance offers a new possibility to convert and to recover the grace of justification. The Fathers of the Church present this sacrament as "the second plank [of salvation] after the shipwreck which is the loss of grace" (Tertullian, *Penance,* 4,2) (*Catechism,* 1446).

1 What is the biblical basis for the sacrament of penance (reconciliation)?

Jesus reconciled us to God by the mystery of his death and resurrection (Rom 5:10). He commissioned the apostles to continue this ministry in the church, saying, "Receive the Holy Spirit. If you forgive the sins of any, they are forgiven them; if you retain the sins of any, they are retained" (Jn 20:22-23).

2 Why is penance valuable for us?

Human weakness marks our daily faith journey. When we sin, we either break or weaken our friendship with God and others. We do, however, belong to a healing, forgiving community, and we stand under the sign of Christ's forgiveness.

Thus, Christians who sin after baptism may be reconciled to God and the church, renewing themselves in the Lord's grace. The good news of forgiveness begets in us an unshakable confidence in the triumph of Jesus' mercy. St. Paul tells us, "... where sin increased, grace abounded all the more ..." (Rom 5:20).

3 Why is reconciliation with the church, as well as with God, important?

While sin disrupts our relationship with God, it also affects how we relate to the Christian community. Sin is not only a failure to love God. It is also a failure to act in a loving, just and merciful way toward our neighbor. Hence, the sacrament of penance involves reconciliation with our brothers and sisters as well as with God.

4 What are the major elements of the Rite of Reconciliation?

The major elements are conversion, confession, act of penance and absolution. They are described as follows:

Conversion: This process involves the inner awareness that we have become alienated from God and one another. We regret such behavior, and state our intention to be restored in love.

Pope Paul VI tells us that "We can only approach the kingdom of Christ by metanoia (conversion). This is a profound change of the whole person ..."

Confession: Confession of sins to a priest is an essential element of this sacrament. Even apart from the sacrament, confessing our sins to others is a liberating experience and facilitates our reconciliation with others. Through confessing our sins, we confront our moral state, take responsibility for our sins, open ourselves anew to God and make a new future possible. We should confess whatever mortal sins we have committed. Though not strictly necessary, we are encouraged by the church to confess venial sins to help us form our consciences, struggle against evil tendencies and make progress in the life of grace.

Act of penance: This action is a symbol of our change in moral attitude, our conversion. It is a sign of a fresh start in our moral and spiritual lives. The confessor may assign as a penance: prayer, works of mercy, service to neighbor, voluntary privation, sacrifices and above all the patient acceptance of the cross we must bear. Such penances make us more like Christ who alone atoned for our sins. We suffer with him that we may be like him. The priest will also ask the penitent to recite an act of contrition.

Absolution: The confessor invites the penitent to pray with him. He then extends his hand(s) over the penitent and recites the words of absolution. The essential text is, "God, the Father of mercies, through the death and resurrection of his Son has reconciled the world to himself and sent the Holy Spirit among us for the forgiveness of sins. Through the ministry of the church, may God give you pardon and peace, and I absolve you from your sins, in the name of the Father, and of the Son and the Holy Spirit." The person responds, "Amen."

5 How does someone receive the sacrament of penance today?

There are three ways to receive the sacrament in the church today. The first is the Rite of Reconciliation for individual penitents, or individual confession, which is most like our past practice of confession. Secondly, penance can be administered in a communal service, which also includes individual confessions. Thirdly, church members may receive penance in a service that includes general absolution. But this last form is only permitted in cases of grave necessity (read the *Catechism*, 1483-84, for the further explanation of when general absolution is permitted).

6 What is a communal penance service?

Communal penance services are occasionally held to emphasize our need to reconcile with the church community as well as with God. Normally, the communal rite includes prayers, Scripture readings, hymns, a homily, an examination of conscience and a call for the blessing of the Spirit. Individual confession and absolution are part of this service.

7 What is general absolution?

With the approval of the local bishop, general absolution may be given in special circumstances. This is usually done when there is a large crowd of people and an insufficient number of confessors. The church, however, asks anyone in serious sin to make an individual confession as soon as possible in order to receive personal guidance and the personal assurance of Christ's forgiveness.

8 Why does the church require individual confession to a priest?

Individual confession has been a tradition since the church's early history. Personal contact with Christ, who addresses each sinner with the words of forgiveness, is the most significant reason for individual confession. It is an expression of the forgiveness and reconciliation present in the community of Jesus' followers. Other reasons for individual confession include:

■ a) We are called to identify and admit our sinfulness, facilitating our efforts for positive change in our lives. By identifying specific sins in our lives, we increase the opportunity for true repentance.

> *Jesus is the doctor of our souls and bodies.*

■ b) The priest is the minister of God's forgiveness, healing and love. This gives us an opportunity to hear the words of forgiveness, as well as to receive spiritual counseling. It is a special blessing of the sacrament of penance.

■ c) Because of our sin we must reconcile with the Lord and our community. We should recall that reconciliation with God is of first and utmost importance. "The whole power of the sacrament of Penance consists in restoring us to God's grace and joining us with him in an intimate friendship" (*Catechism*, 1468).

The priest, as the representative of our church community, helps us to fulfill that requirement. The priest acts in the person of Christ. In this role, the priest not only "helps" but effects reconciliation with the Lord and with the church.

9 What are some fundamental elements in the building up of our moral lives?

You will live a better moral life when you keep these matters in mind.

■ 1. You should live the two laws of Jesus: (a) Love God with all your mind, heart and strength. (b) Love your neighbor as yourself and as Jesus has loved you.

■ 2. Remember you are an image of God. (a) This means you can know the truth. (b) You can will the good. (c) You can act freely—but always in reference to truth and goodness. (d) You have been given human dignity by God and this is the real source of your self worth. (e) You are a person in communion, meaning you must always be aware of others' needs and hopes and give them your love, care and concern. These five qualities characterize you as God's image. Live them and you will be moral.

■ 3. Practice virtue in order to be moral. Unless we acquire good habits or virtues, we will have a hard time being moral. Without virtue, we need to reinvent the wheel when facing each challenge.

■ 4. Pray for the seven gifts of the Spirit so that you can have divine help in acquiring the virtues.

■ 5. Be aware of the reality of sin, both mortal sin which destroys our relationship with God and others, and venial sin which weakens this relationship.

■ 6. Inform and form your conscience.

10 How do we form our conscience?

The church teaches, "Let your conscience be your guide." But the church also teaches that this must be an informed and formed conscience. Our consciences are not the source of moral standards. That source comes from God. Conscience makes judgments in reference to God's laws. Here are the reference points for conscience formation:

■ 1. *The Natural Law.* Natural law is a reflection of the eternal law. God plants the natural law in our hearts when he creates us. Within our deepest being is a light that comes from God's eternal law and glows within us.

■ 2. *The Ten Commandments.* In case we miss the natural law in our hearts, God has revealed to us the ten commandments, which are specifications of this law. If we want to know what the eternal law requires, we should obey the commandments. They are not burdens because they are meant for human good, fulfillment and achievement of proper destiny. What burdens us are the sins forbidden by the commandments. We either control greed or greed controls us. We either control alcohol and drugs or they enslave us. We either control sex or it controls us.

■ 3. ***The Teachings of Christ.*** Jesus taught us the two laws of love of God and love of neighbor. These love laws are calls to covenant with and discipleship with Jesus. His Sermon on the Mount and Last Supper Discourse specify what this means. His beatitudes are calls to personal happiness because they show what our attitudinal life should be. His way of the cross and resurrection illustrate its actual practice. Jesus was a moral teacher who showed us how to do it and gave us the grace to make it possible in our lives.

■ 4. ***The Teaching of the Church's Magisterium.*** Jesus gave the apostles the authority to carry on his message and mission. They passed that on to the popes and bishops. Jesus gave them the Spirit to guide them in truth and be moral teachers in the church. They do not invent moral teachings, but apply the teachings of Christ to various situations as they arise in history.

■ 5. ***The Holy Spirit.*** See John 16:8. The Holy Spirit forms our consciences by convincing us of our sinfulness, convicting us of it, converting us from it and consoling us in the process.

These five steps are sure guides for forming our consciences.

> *I*n the ten commandments we have a practical framework of covenant love in action.

11 How can the ten commandments help us in forming our conscience?

In the ten commandments we have a practical framework of covenant love in action. They are guides for conscience formation. We can be guided by the negative aspect of each, which forbids undesirable behavior, as well as a positive aspect, which is central to enhancing our union with God and our community.

■ 1. You shall honor no other God but me.
Against idolatry of self, others or the state.
For faith in a loving and forgiving God.

■ 2. You shall not misuse the name of the Lord, your God.

Against irreverence for God and people or making light of the mystery of their relationship.
For the reverence and value of the mystery of God and human beings.

■ 3. You shall keep holy the sabbath day.
Against refusal to acknowledge our dependence on God's love and mercy and providential care for all creation.
For a proper observance of the Christian Sunday by attendance at the Eucharist, attention to family nurturing and rest from our labors.

■ 4. You shall honor your father and mother.
Against any force or influence that weakens or destroys family life.
For behavior that builds strong, Christian family life.

■ 5. You shall not kill.
Against those who deny or destroy the sacredness of human life by murder, torture, abortion, euthanasia, etc.
For the honoring of every human life as sacred.

■ 6. You shall not commit adultery.
Against dehumanizing sexuality and irreverence to the marriage vow of fidelity. Sins include adultery, fornication, homosexual acts, incest, masturbation, divorce and pornography.
For human dignity and fulfillment in light of covenant love, fidelity in marriage, chastity and the positive role of sexuality in marital love.

■ 7. You shall not steal.
Against stealing personal property, including exploitation of the poor.
For protection of personal property and economic justice for poor and oppressed people.

■ 8. You shall not bear false witness against your neighbor.
Against lying, cheating and defamation of character.
For the values of truth and honesty in society.

■ 9. You shall not covet your neighbor's wife.
Against lust and the permission of disordered passions.
For the value of humans as worthy of love and reverence, coupled with respect for the marriage vows.

■ 10. You shall not covet your neighbor's goods.
Against greed, avarice or exploitation of the environment.
For wholesome love of creation, poverty of spirit and loving care for the world's environment.

"ARE ANY AMONG YOU SICK?" (JAMES 5:14)

"Are any among you sick? They should call for the elders of the church and have them pray over them, anointing them with oil in the name of the Lord. The prayer of faith will save the sick, and the Lord will raise them up; and anyone who has committed sins will be forgiven. Therefore confess your sins to one another, and pray for one another, so that you may be healed" (Jas 5:14-16).

In the liturgical tradition of both East and West there is testimony from ancient times about the anointing of the sick with blessed oil. Over the centuries the anointing of the sick was conferred more and more exclusively on those at the verge of death. Because of this it received the name of Extreme Unction. In spite of this evolution the liturgy never neglected to pray for the recovery of health for the sick if that would be helpful for their salvation.

At Vatican II, the bishops recommended calling it the sacrament of anointing of the sick, because it "... is not a sacrament for those only who are at the point of death. Hence, as soon as any one of the faithful begins to be in danger of death from sickness or old age, the appropriate time for him to receive this sacrament has certainly already arrived" (*Liturgy*, 73).

"Are any among you sick?" (*James* 5:14)

■ A. What is the sacrament of anointing of the sick?
The sacrament of Anointing of the Sick is given to those who are seriously ill by anointing them on the forehead and hands with duly blessed oil—pressed from olives or from other plants—saying, only once: "Through this holy anointing may the Lord in his love and mercy help you with the grace of the Holy Spirit. May the Lord who frees you from sin save you and raise you up" (*Catechism*, 1513).

■ B. Why do we speak of Christ as a physician?
Christ's compassion toward the sick and his many healings of every kind of infirmity are a resplendent sign that "God has visited his people" (*Lk* 7:16) and that the Kingdom of God is close at hand. Jesus has the power not only to heal, but also to forgive sins; he has come to heal the whole man, soul and body; he is the physician the sick have need of. His compassion toward all who suffer goes so far that he identifies himself with them: "I was sick and you visited me" (*Mt* 25:36). His preferential love for the sick has not ceased through the centuries to draw the very special attention of Christians toward all those who suffer in body and soul. It is the source of tireless efforts to comfort them (*Catechism*, 1503).

■ C. What is the role of suffering in human life?
Illness and suffering have always been among the gravest problems confronted in human life. In illness, man experiences his powerlessness, his limitations, and his finitude. Every illness can make us glimpse death.

Illness can lead to anguish, self-absorption, sometimes even despair and revolt against God. It can also make a person more mature, helping him discern in his life what is not essential so that he can turn toward that which is. Very often illness provokes a search for God and a return to him (*Catechism*, 1500-1501).

1 What is the purpose of the sacrament of the anointing of the sick?

This sacrament is designed to give comfort to the sick and to help them to reconcile themselves to God and the church. In addition, it serves to help the person to have a strong, positive faith attitude and it assists in physical, mental and spiritual healing.

2 How is the sacrament of the sick administered?

A priest lays his hands over the forehead of the person and anoints him or her with oil. Doing so, he prays, "Through this holy anointing may the

> *Very often illness provokes a search for God and a return to him.*

Lord in his love and mercy help you with the grace of the Holy Spirit. May the Lord who frees you from sin save you and raise you up."

3 What is the communal celebration of the sacrament of anointing?

Whenever possible, the anointing of the sick should take place in a communal setting. In this ceremony, the church recommends the sick to the Lord, who himself has suffered and been glorified. The attending priest then prays for the relief and salvation of the sick, who are asked to associate themselves with the passion and death of Christ. In this manner, the sick make their contribution to the good of God's people.

4 What is the sick person's role in the communal celebration of the sacrament?

The community recognizes that a person's illness frequently prevents him or her from having a fulfilling role in the activities of society or the church. However, it is possible for an ill person to participate in Jesus' redemptive suffering, as a reminder to each of us of the limitations of our earthly lives and our eternal destiny.

5 How does an individual's suffering affect the church?

Sick people can be a curse or a blessing to those with whom they come in contact. Much depends on the patient's attitude toward suffering. Some approach illness with stoic endurance. Others face illness with spiritual composure, identifying their pain with Jesus' passion and offering their own suffering for the salvation of mankind. Pope John

XXIII, for example, offered his final, physical agonies of illness for the conversion of the Russian people to Christianity.

At the same time, illness challenges those who care for the sick. Nurses, doctors, family members, friends, clergy and religious are challenged to approach the sick person in a total healing manner, providing physical, mental, emotional and spiritual assistance. Similarly, rare and incurable diseases challenge researchers to find cures.

6 Can sickness be productive?

Illness and pain can teach us many lessons. For example, illness often teaches a person who has had a heart attack to adopt a lifestyle more in harmony with his or her physical limits. Pain and death can be accepted as a positive witness to one's beliefs and convictions. Numerous saints endured physical torment and death in witness to their boundless faith in Jesus, who suffered and died for our salvation.

The most relevant aspect of sickness and pain is the attitude we bring to our suffering. For some people, sickness produces spiritual growth. A sick person who exhibits nobility of spirit while enduring great pain is an inspiration to us all. Christian mystics often teach us that they identify their trials with Christ's passion for the continuation of the Lord's redeeming work.

7 Can illness be a temptation?

Illness is normally a trial or test. The pain and tedium of sickness can induce tendencies to self-pity, remorse and even despair. Sometimes we can be tempted to curse God for our misfortune. At the same time, grave illness can be an occasion of deepening our faith in the Lord and an opportunity to grow in spiritual love.

Still, it should be noted that some illness can be avoided by positive health care. Jesus and the apostles devoted much time to healing the sick (Lk 7:20-23; 9:1-6).

8 What is the relationship of illness to our moral lives?

During times of grave illness, some people think God is cruel and unsympathetic. In New Testament days, there were those who believed physical affliction was primarily the result of sin. In the story of Job, people spoke of Job's sorrows as a deserved punishment from God for his sins.

When questioned about illness and its relation to sin, Jesus rejected these views (Jn 9:1-3).

The church teaches that suffering may be the result of sinfulness, especially with respect to arrogance and perversity. Suffering can also be the result of our moral and spiritual commitment, as in the case of Christ's passion and the witness of the martyrs.

9 How should Catholics prepare for death?

Catholics should prepare for death by living each day of their lives as though it were the last. The best way to do this is to lead a life that allows the person to grow both morally and spiritually. Therefore, Catholics should reject ideas which deny their mortality, especially those which prohibit deepening of their faith in eternal life with God.

> *Whenever possible, the anointing of the sick should take place in a communal setting.*

As death draws near people who are ill should work towards a peaceful acceptance of this inevitable fact. This process should also involve an identification with Jesus' redemptive suffering and death. A dying Catholic should meditate on Christ's attitude of forgiveness on the cross, his care for others and his endless generosity. Having worked through the period of darkness, the person should commend himself or herself to the Father, as did our Lord.

The sacrament of the sick is an "anointing unto glory." Viaticum is Eucharist for the journey to eternal life. Thus, a well-prepared Catholic comes to life's final moment as a time of spiritual consummation and beginning.

10 What are the last rites?

The last rites refer to three sacraments or rites in the Catholic Church, which are received by a person near death. The three rites are reconciliation (sacrament of penance), the anointing of the sick and Eucharist (here called Viaticum, or food for the journey).

It should be noted that none of these rites is reserved solely for the dying. Reconciliation and Eucharist are part of the ongoing life of a Catholic, while anointing the sick may be administered as soon as a person is discovered to have a serious illness.

11 Why should a priest be called at the time of a Catholic's death?

A priest is called so that, as a representative of the church, he may pray along with the dying person and family members and administer the sacrament of anointing. The following prayer is taken from the Rite for Anointing of the Sick:

"My brother (or sister) in faith, I entrust you to God who created you. May you return to the one who formed you from dust of this earth. May Mary, the angels and all the saints come to meet you as you go forth from this life.

"May Christ, who was crucified for you, bring you freedom and peace. May Christ, the Son of God, who died for you, take you into his kingdom. May Christ, the Good Shepherd, give you a place within his flock. May he forgive your sins and keep you among his people. May you see your Redeemer face to face and enjoy the sight of God forever."

12 How are the last rites administered?

First, the sacrament of reconciliation is administered to a person who is willing and able to receive it. Then, the sacrament of anointing the sick is given, either by anointing several senses or only the person's forehead. Lastly, Viaticum (Eucharist) is given to the sick person.

When someone is unconscious, the sacraments of penance and anointing may be given conditionally or without the person's active participation. If the person has already died, a priest or other church representative prays for the peaceful journey of the deceased and brings comfort to family members.

13 How does the sacrament of the sick relate to faith healing?

There are some similarities between the sacrament of the sick and faith healing. For example, both experiences seek to improve the health of the sick person. Each event demands strong faith on the part of the sick person and both usually take place in a community setting.

14 What do Catholics believe about faith healing?

Catholics accept the gift of healing, as it is frequently mentioned in the New Testament. It is believed to be a charism of the Holy Spirit given to some individuals for the benefit of the whole community. We should not be surprised when miracles occur today through Jesus' power, as shown in the charismatic healing ministry.

> *Family members and friends can share Jesus' healing power with loved ones through daily care, patience and love.*

Abuses have, however, occurred among Christians in the name of faith healing. Some "healings" are staged events to increase credibility. Sometimes, healings are temporary and seem to be simply the result of an elevated emotional state. People who truly possess this gift have a responsibility to exercise it humbly for the purpose of building the community of God.

15 Who has the gift of healing?

The gift of healing is not only given to those who are involved in charismatic groups or healing services. Rather, it is the inspiration and power behind all who minister to the sick in the name of Jesus Christ. For example, health care professionals can recognize God's power in their work to conquer disease. Lay and ordained people working in health care ministries can bring spiritual and community support to the ill.

Finally, family members and friends can share Jesus' healing power with loved ones through daily care, patience and love.

16 What does it mean to be healed?

The usual connotation of the word implies physical healing. In these cases, people who could not walk are now able to walk; those diagnosed with cancer find that tumors have disappeared; and people with constant arthritic pain are freed from their suffering.

This, however, is not the only meaning of the word healed. Often, people pray for physical healing at shrines such as the one at Lourdes or with a person who has the charismatic gift of healing or in personal prayer. Though there may not be physical healing, they frequently experience a return to deep peace, that provides them with a blessed acceptance of suffering with an understanding of its redemptive power. In addition, freedom from the moral sickness of sin that keeps us from closeness with the Lord also is a real healing.

17 Does the sacrament of the sick bring healing?

The purpose of the sacrament is expressed in the prayer for the blessing of the oil used in the rite, which reads, "May your blessing come upon all who are anointed with this oil, that they may be freed from pain and illness and made well again in body, mind and soul. Father, may this oil be blessed for our use in the name of our Lord, Jesus Christ, who lives and reigns with you forever and ever. Amen."

The church teaches that each person who receives this sacrament experiences God's healing power in their lives. This is why the sacrament is for all who are seriously sick.

"WHAT GOD HAS JOINED TOGETHER…"(MATTHEW 19:6)

"How can I ever express the happiness of a marriage joined together by the Church, strengthened by an offering, sealed by a blessing, announced by angels and ratified by the Father? … How wonderful the bond between two believers, one in hope, one in desire, one in discipline, one in the same service! They are both children of the one Father and servants of the same Master, undivided in spirit and flesh. They are truly two in one flesh and where the flesh is one, one also is the spirit" (Tertullian, *To His Wife*, 2, 8, 6-7).

In Ireland, there is a ring called the claddagh. The ring has hands folded in prayer, a heart signifying love and a crown which proclaims lasting fidelity. The claddagh is the ring of loyalty and reminds the wearer that prayer, love and fidelity are the foundations of a lasting marriage.

Through Scripture we learn that God's covenant with us is one of everlasting love and fidelity. His "marriage" to us is a source of grace for men and women who have embraced the sacrament of marriage.

Marriage Serves the Communion of the Church, the Family and Society

■ A. How does marriage fit in God's plan?

Sacred Scripture begins with the creation of man and woman in the image and likeness of God and concludes with a vision of "the wedding-feast of the Lamb" (*Gn* 1:26-27; *Rv* 19:7,9). Scripture speaks throughout of marriage and its "mystery," its institution and the meaning God has given it, its origin and its end, its various realizations throughout the history of salvation, the difficulties arising from sin and its renewal "in the Lord" in the New Covenant of Christ and the Church (*Catechism*, 1602).

■ B. Who are the ministers of the sacrament of marriage?

In the Latin Church, it is ordinarily understood that the spouses, as ministers of Christ's grace, mutually confer upon each other the sacrament of Matrimony by expressing their consent before the Church. In the Eastern liturgies the minister of this sacrament (which is called "Crowning") is the priest or bishop who, after receiving the mutual consent of the spouses, successively crowns the bridegroom and the bride as a sign of the marriage covenant (*Catechism*, 1623).

■ C. What is the role of fidelity in marriage?

By its very nature, conjugal love requires the inviolable fidelity of the spouses. This is the consequence of the gift of themselves which they make to each other. Love seeks to be definitive; it cannot be an arrangement "until further notice." The "intimate union of marriage, as a mutual giving of two persons, and the good of the children, demand total fidelity from the spouses and require an unbreakable union between them" (*Modern World*, 48) (*Catechism*, 1646).

1 What is the biblical basis for the sacrament of marriage?

Scripture tells us that God said, "It is not good that the man should be alone; I will make him a helper as his partner" (Gn 2:18). When Eve was brought to Adam, he remarked, "This at last is bone of my bones and flesh of my flesh …" (Gn 2:23). Genesis tells us that "Therefore a man leaves his father and his mother and clings to his wife, and they become one flesh" (2:24).

2 What does Scripture tell us is the purpose of marriage?

Once the man and woman had been brought together, the Bible tells us that the Lord instructed them to "Be fruitful and multiply ..." (Gn 1:28). Therefore, we learn that marriage is divinely established. We also are told that it is a matter of bonded love between a husband and wife, oriented essentially toward the raising of a family.

3 How does Christ relate to marriage in the New Testament?

Christ's presence at the marriage feast at Cana is the announcement that he is present in all Christian weddings, giving them a sacramental value (Jn 2:1-11). Jesus established the sacrament of marriage so that men and women may be united with him and receive his grace.

> *How wonderful the bond between two believers, one in hope, one in desire, one in discipline, one in the same service!*

Therefore, the couple is united both to one another and to Jesus in marriage. Scripture tells us that the love between husband and wife should be modeled after Jesus' love for us (Eph 5:22-23).

4 What is the sacrament of marriage?

Marriage is the sacrament whereby a baptized man and woman freely, legally and in faith surrender themselves to each other and to Christ. It is a permanent union, bonded by the power and grace of Jesus. The couple will begin to experience this power as they take their vows (promises) in the presence of the priest or deacon and the believing community.

Sacramental married life begins with these promises and continues throughout the life-long relationship of the couple.

5 What is the role of the priest or deacon in the marriage ceremony?

The priest or deacon officially witnesses the sacrament of marriage and blesses the couple in the name of the church. It is, however, the man and woman who actually *minister* the sacrament to one another in the Latin church (cf. Question B above).

6 Are the marriage promises expected to be permanent?

The church expects the marital promises to be kept for life. A permanent union will help assure both stability and continuity in the raising of a family and keep the couple together in troubled times.

All love relationships have their ups and downs. Permanent commitment motivates couples to work toward strengthening their love amidst hardship. Just as Jesus does not divorce the church, nor break his promise of fidelity, neither should husbands and wives break their promises to each other.

7 What is the church's position on divorce?

The Catholic Church holds that there is no divorce or remarriage for her members. The New Testament tells us that when asked about divorce, Jesus declared, "What God has joined together, let no one separate" (Mt 19:3-9).

Further testimony is given by St. Paul, who said, "... the wife should not separate from her husband (but if she does separate, let her remain unmarried or else be reconciled to her husband), and that the husband should not divorce his wife" (1 Cor 7:10, 11).

8 Is divorce permitted in light of "lewd conduct," as mentioned in Scripture?

In Matthew's Gospel, chapter 19, we find the Pharisees questioning Jesus on marriage and divorce. Jesus replied that divorce was no longer permitted, save where *unchastity* is involved (19:9). Catholic biblical scholars teach that here Christ is referring to incestuous relationships among blood relatives and not adultery between a married couple. An incestuous union would not be sanctioned; therefore, the parties could separate and marry.

9 Does the church ever allow members to obtain a legal divorce?

In exceptional cases the church permits Catholics to obtain divorces but not to remarry. A local bishop may judge that certain couples may seek a legal divorce or separation to determine child support, custody, alimony and distribution of property. The couple would be cautioned that remarriage is not permitted.

10 How does the church view marriages of non-Catholics?

The church considers the marriages of non-Catholics to be real and valid until death. This assumes that the marriage was entered into freely and legally and that the couple intended to remain married to one another.

11 What is the Pauline Privilege?

The Pauline Privilege is the application of a principle concerning the marriage of two unbaptized persons, one of whom becomes a Christian after the marriage has taken place (cf. 1 Cor 7:12-16).

Under this rule, a real and valid union may be dissolved in favor of the faith even though the marriage has been consummated.

12 What are annulments?

In annulment cases, the church judges that no real and valid marriage ever existed. People granted annulments are free to marry again.

13 What are the conditions for annulments?

Some possible reasons for annulments are: when it can be proven that the couple had no intention of having children; the couple never intended to have a permanent union; and one or both partners did not intend to remain faithful. It should be noted that there are other reasons for annulment besides these.

14 Are psychological factors ever considered in annulment cases?

Sometimes psychological factors are considered. However, applicants must demonstrate that a condition existed at the time of the marriage that gravely impaired the mind and/or will of one or both partners. Extensive investigation is required in these cases.

If an annulment is granted, partners may be free to marry, provided the conditions for granting the annulment no longer exist. In the cases of both the Pauline Privilege and annulments, the church provides diocesan marriage counseling and a staff of experts to judge the eligibility of the applicants. The process should normally be initiated with the parish priest, who can make an initial assessment of the case and advise the couple about the next steps.

15 What preparations are couples expected to make before their wedding?

Although the content of each may vary, some type of marriage instruction is required by all dioceses. Through the local parish, the church community wishes to communicate its expectations about marriage to the couple.

In addition, these instructions are designed to inspire the partners to dedicate themselves to the values of love, caring, affection and sacrifice that will help them to form a happy and successful marriage.

16 What are the church's teachings about pre-marital and extra-marital sex?

The church teaches that sex outside of marriage is wrong. Sexual intercourse is meant to be a sign of the permanent, loving commitment between a man and woman, and marriage is the sacrament (and institution) in which the commitment is meant to take place.

When people engage in pre-marital sex (fornication), they are acting outside of a permanent commitment to each other. The greatest gift a man and woman bring to each other at marriage is their love, of which virginity is a sign.

Any spouse who seeks sex outside of marriage commits adultery, because this partner is acting disloyally to his or her spouse. The permanent promise of fidelity made by both at the marriage ceremony is now broken. The greatest gift a couple offers throughout marriage is love, of which sexual fidelity is a sign.

17 What about couples living together outside of marriage?

The church believes in marriage! The sacrament of marriage brings with it the help couples need to live out the difficult task of maintaining a loving, committed relationship throughout their lives. The marriage commitment is essential for stability and growth for the couple and the family that will result from this union.

18 What does the church say about mixed marriages?

A mixed marriage is between a Catholic and a non-Catholic, who may be baptized or unbaptized. Express permission of ecclesiastical authority is required for the liceity of marriage between a Catholic and a baptized non-Catholic; an express dispensation is required for the validity of a marriage between a Catholic and an unbaptized non-Catholic (cf. *Catechism,* 1635).

The church prefers that Catholics marry within our religion, so as to uphold the harmony of mutual belief and assure a common value system in raising children. In a mixed marriage, there are likely to be serious differences about prayer, church attendance, education of children and morals and values. Sometimes partners in a mixed marriage unfortunately push religion out of the picture for the sake of peace in the home. In other situations, the faith of both the Catholic and the non-Catholic partner continues as a vibrant part of the marriage through the grace of the Holy Spirit.

19 In what cases are mixed marriages likely to be successful?

Where people are sensitive and understanding partners and loving parents, mixed marriages can and have worked well. It is, however, beneficial if people discuss the possible difficulties of a mixed marriage *before* the marriage takes place. In this way the couple can develop a true appreciation of what is ahead.

20 What is the church's position on abortion?

The church teaches that human life begins at conception; therefore, any effort to destroy life is the killing of an innocent person. The church teaches that an unborn child has the "right to life." Abortion is seen as more than an academic debate—life itself is at stake.

In support of this position, the church advocates programs that provide funds and services to women involved in unwanted pregnancies. In many cases agencies arrange for adoptions and provide counseling for the mother, if it is desired. Acceptance of abortion at the beginning of life, the church fears, would widen the possibilities for acceptance of active euthanasia (mercy killing) at the end of life.

21 What is the church's teaching on artificial contraception and family planning?

The church approves of natural family planning, in which no mechanical or artificial device is used in the sex act. This is a plan that involves periodic discipline. Couples should seek the advice of a doctor and counseling from natural family planning agencies available in their diocese. In addition, spiritual strength should be acquired by means of prayer and participation in the eucharistic celebration.

Pope Paul VI restated the church's official opposition to artificial birth control in his encyclical *Humane Vitae (Of Human Life)*, a position that has been reiterated by Pope John Paul II. The popes teach that every act of sexual intercourse should be open to the possibility of creating human life. Therefore, the introduction of artificial means to prevent conception is both unnatural and wrong.

Reflection:
There is clearly a restrictive side to many of the church's moral standards regarding marriage and family life. Included in these standards are positions on divorce, adultery, fornication, mixed marriages, contraception and abortion. At the same time, church teachings enhance the true meaning of love and support a growing relationship.

The restrictive aspect of the law does, however, have a positive value orientation. That is, it teaches that real marriage reflects the intensity of God's love for us. The more glorious the marital and family love, the more truly is marriage a sacrament revealing God's love.

The church's challenge to us is not as much to avoid breaking the law, as it is to intensify loving family relationships. While the church advises discipline and self-control, her chief message to us is that we should aspire to achieve greater self-surrender and self-abandonment to each other. The purpose of the marriage laws is to free couples and families for the adventure of love and the good of children. Freedom from infidelity is freedom for fidelity and the pleasure and magnificence of loyalty.

Jesus is the third partner in all sacramental marriages. He toasts the couple with the wine of his affection and draws them into a love that is truly forever.

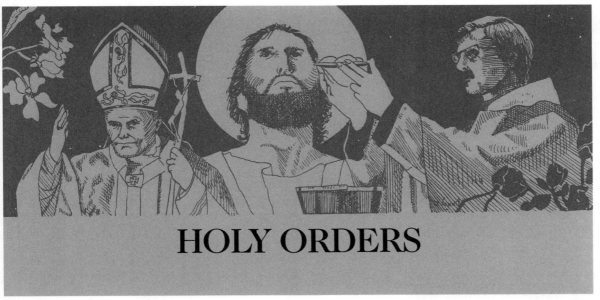

HOLY ORDERS

"Who then is the priest? He is the defender of truth, who stands with the angels, gives glory with archangels, causes sacrifices to rise to the altar on high, shares Christ's priesthood, refashions creation, restores it in God's image, recreates it for the world on high and, even greater, is divinized and divinizes" (St. Gregory Nazianzen, *Prayer*, 73-74).

"The priest continues the work of redemption on earth ... If we really understood the priest on earth, we would not die of fright but of love ... The Priesthood is the love of the heart of Jesus" (St. John Vianney, quoted in B. Nodet's *Jean-Marie Vianney*, 100).

"Lord, fill with the gift of the Holy Spirit him whom you have deigned to raise to the rank of priesthood, that he might be worthy to stand without reproach before your altar, to proclaim the Gospel of your kingdom, to fulfill the ministry of your word of truth, to offer you spiritual gifts and sacrifices, to renew your people by the bath of rebirth so that he may go out to meet our great God and Savior Jesus Christ, your only Son, on the day of his Second Coming, and may receive from your vast goodness the recompense of a faithful administration of his order" (Byzantine Liturgy, *Euchologian*).

Holy Orders

■ A. Why is this sacrament called orders?
The word *order* in Roman antiquity designated an established civil body, especially a governing body. *Ordinatio* means incorporation into an *ordo*. In the Church there are established bodies which Tradition, not without a basis in Sacred Scripture, has since ancient times called *taxeis* (Greek) or *ordines*. And so the liturgy speaks of the *ordo episcoporum,* the *ordo presbyterorum,* the *ordo diaconorum.* Other groups also receive this name of *ordo:* catechumens, virgins, spouses, widows, ...

Integration into one of these bodies in the Church was accomplished by a rite called *ordinatio*, a religious and liturgical act which was a consecration, a blessing or a sacrament. Today the word *"ordination"* is reserved for the sacramental act which integrates a man into the order of bishops, presbyters, or deacons, and goes beyond a simple *election, designation, delegation,* or *institution* by the community, for it confers a gift of the Holy Spirit that permits the exercise of a "sacred power" (*sacra potestas)* which can come only from Christ himself through his Church (*Catechism*, 1537-1538).

■ B. What is the relation of ordained priesthood and the common priesthood of all the baptized?
But "the members do not all have the same function." Certain members are called by God, in and through the Church, to a special service of the community. These servants are chosen and consecrated by the sacrament of Holy Orders, by which the Holy Spirit enables them to act in the person of Christ the head, for the service of all the members of the Church. The ordained minister is, as it were, an "icon" of Christ the priest (*Catechism,* 1142).

■ C. In what sense do the two priesthoods differ?
While the common priesthood of the faithful is exercised by the unfolding of baptismal grace—a life of faith, hope, and charity, a life according to the Spirit—the ministerial priesthood is at the service of the common priesthood. It is directed at the unfolding of the baptismal grace of all Christians. The ministerial priesthood is a *means* by which Christ unceasingly builds up and leads his Church. For this reason it is transmitted by its own sacrament, the sacrament of Holy Orders (*Catechism,* 1547).

1 What is the priesthood?

The Epistle to the Hebrews speaks of the priesthood in the following way: "Every high priest chosen from among mortals is put in charge of things pertaining to God on their behalf, to offer gifts and sacrifices for sins. He is able to deal gently with the ignorant and wayward, since he himself is subject to weakness; and because of this he must offer sacrifice for his own sins as well as for those of the people" (Heb 5:1-3).

> *T*he priest is a mediator presenting offerings of love and surrender to God.

The priest is, therefore, a mediator presenting offerings of love and surrender to God, in the person of Christ and in the name of the community of believers. At the same time, he is chosen by God to communicate the Lord's gifts of grace, love and forgiveness to the community.

2 How was Jesus Christ "ordained" a priest?

When the Son of God became a human being, he took complete possession of his humanity. The moment of his incarnation or "ordination" was the moment of Jesus' priestly consecration. Incarnation marked Jesus forever as the one eternal mediator between God and human beings. On the feast of Christmas, we behold the One who "... anointed you with the oil of gladness ..." (Heb 1:9).

Jesus *is* priest. Bishops, priests and deacons have no priestly meaning apart from his ministry. He is *the* source for the entire priesthood, which praises God and develops according to the Lord's plan.

3 What is the sacrament of holy orders?

In the sacrament of holy orders, Jesus, through the church's bishops, calls a man to be a bishop, presbyter or deacon to share in the priesthood of Christ. Bishops and presbyters act in the person of Christ by offering the sacrifice of the Eucharist, hearing confessions, anointing the sick, teaching and preaching God's word and shepherding the baptized toward the kingdom of God and in their role of sanctifying the world.

4 What is the major mission of bishops, priests and deacons?

God calls them to bring Jesus to the world through word, sacrament and service. When preaching the word of salvation (Gospel), they are to be the light of the world. In celebrating the sacraments, they must be the *salt* of the earth, with hearts full of tenderness and forgiveness for the community. They are to pattern their lives after Jesus, reflecting the goals of the Lord in establishing the kingdom of love, justice and mercy.

5 What are the different holy orders?

There are three orders, and they are as follows:
- a) *Bishops:* They are the successors of the apostles and can represent Christ in the ministry of all the sacraments. Only bishops may administer holy orders, and they are normally the ministers of confirmation.
- b) *Priests:* Priests are involved in the ministry of preaching and service to the community. They may celebrate the Eucharist, and the sacraments of penance, anointing of the sick, baptism and occasionally confirmation.
- c) *Deacons:* Ordained by a bishop, deacons can baptize, distribute communion, witness marriages, preach and engage in works of service to the community of the faithful. Vatican II established a permanent diaconate that can include married as well as celibate men.

6 What is the principal sacramental action for a priest?

The priestly ministry reaches its summit in the celebration of the Eucharist, which is the source and center of the church's unity. Only a bishop or priest is able to act in the person of Christ in presiding over and effecting—by the power of the Spirit—a sacrificial meal, the Eucharist, wherein the People of God are associated in Christ's saving sacrifice.

7 How are we to view the full context of priestly ministry?

The Synod of Bishops on the Priesthood places the priest's ministry in celebrating Eucharist at the summit of his calling. This is, however, to be in the context of his ministry of the other sacraments and his call to proclaim the word of God and gather together the community of the faithful.

In proclaiming the word, priests are to strengthen the living community and evangelize those not yet members of the Body of Christ. In building the community, the priest's primary task is spiritual. Clergy should also strive to have a positive impact on people's civil, political and economic situations.

In addition, priests must attempt to awaken members to Christ's faith, hope and love, so the full spirit of his kingdom may be realized in the human order of our lives.

8 What is the "common priesthood of the faithful"?

The church teaches that at baptism every Catholic becomes a member of the common priesthood of the faithful. By ordination in holy orders, certain persons of the church community become members of the hierarchical or ministerial priesthood.

> *The common priesthood of the faithful and the ministerial or hierarchical priesthood are nonetheless interrelated. Each of them in its own special way is a participation in the one priesthood of Christ.*

The Vatican II fathers tell us that the baptized, "... by regeneration and the anointing of the Holy Spirit, are consecrated into a spiritual house and a holy priesthood ... Though they differ from one another in essence and not only in degree, the common priesthood of the faithful and the minis-

terial or hierarchical priesthood are nonetheless interrelated. Each of them in its own special way is a participation in the one priesthood of Christ" (*Church,* 10).

9 What are the church's hierarchical titles and their meanings?

The hierarchical titles within the Catholic Church are pope, bishop, cardinal, father, monsignor and deacon. Their meanings are as follows:

Pope: This man is the Bishop of Rome, the successor of St. Peter and the spiritual leader of all Roman Catholics.

Bishop: These men are the successors of the apostles and are usually the spiritual leaders of local churches. One or several auxiliary bishops may assist in the ministry. Some local churches with the largest populations and territories are called archdioceses. They are led by archbishops.

Cardinal: This is essentially an honorary title conferred on bishops. Cardinals usually head a large archdiocese or hold a chief administrative position in the church.

Father: This is the general title for priest, given in the spirit of St. Paul who said, "In Christ Jesus I became your father through the gospel" (1 Cor 4:15).

Monsignor: This is an honorary title given to priests for distinguished service to people and the church as a whole.

Deacon: This is the title given to those who are ordained to the permanent diaconate. There is also the "transitional diaconate" given to a man prior to his ordination to priesthood.

10 What is the difference between diocesan and religious priests?

Diocesan priests are clergy who usually work in the diocese under the local bishop. They are bound by the law of celibacy (Latin Rite) and are supported by the diocese. Their chief ministry occurs in parishes. Religious priests belong to communities of men bound by vows of poverty, chastity and obedience to religious superiors. While they may work in parishes, they are usually involved in ministries such as teaching or missionary work.

11   Who are religious?

Religious are men and women who join communities and are bound by the rules of their order. They take vows or promises of poverty, chastity and obedience to superiors. Usually they live in community, sharing prayer, meals and goods, as well as values and goals.

Religious men may be priests or brothers, and religious women are either sisters or nuns. They may reside in convents, monasteries, abbeys or provincial houses.

12   What is the role of bishops in the church?

Bishops are ordained to the highest level of holy orders by the "laying on of hands" by other bishops. They, along with the Bishop of Rome, share the triple office of Christ, that of teaching, ruling and sanctifying the People of God. New bishops are usually selected by the pope, upon the recommendation of those already serving as bishops.

"The individual bishops, who are placed in charge of particular churches, exercise their pastoral government over the portion of the People of God committed to their care, and not over other churches nor over the universal Church. But each of them, as a member of the episcopal college and a legitimate successor of the apostles, is obliged by Christ's decree and command to be solicitous for the whole Church" (*Church*, 23).

13   What is collegiality?

Collegiality refers to the exercise of authority in the church. In the strict sense, collegiality describes the manner in which the body of bishops in communion with the church, together with the pope, exercises its power. It does so solemnly when the bishops gather in ecumenical council with the successor of St. Peter (cf. *Church*, 23, 25). Bishops act in a collegial manner when they exercise their responsibilities while dispersed throughout the world. "Their responsibility also includes concern for all the Churches, with and under the Pope" (*Catechism*, 939; see also 877-887).

14   Is there one area to which Christ calls all members of the church?

Every member of the People of God is called to a life of holiness. Bishops, priests, deacons, religious and laity alike are called to the faith journey that leads to sanctity. "All of Christ's followers, therefore, are invited and bound to pursue holiness and the perfect fulfillment of their proper state ... By this holiness a more human way of life is promoted even in this earthly society ..." (*Church*, 42, 40).

15   Are all priests and bishops required to be celibate?

In the Latin Church, all priests and bishops are called to celibacy. In the Eastern churches, candidates for the priesthood may marry before ordination, but not afterwards. Should priests' wives die, the priests may not remarry. Bishops of the Eastern churches are called to celibacy. They are usually chosen from the ranks of celibate monks.

16   What about the ordination of women?

Only a baptized man *(vir)* validly receives sacred ordination. The Lord Jesus chose men *(viri)* to form the college of the twelve apostles, and the apostles did the same when they chose collaborators to succeed them in their ministry. The college of bishops, with whom the priests are united in the priesthood, makes the college of the twelve an ever-present and ever-active reality until Christ's return. The Church recognizes herself to be bound by this choice made by the Lord himself. For this reason the ordination of women is not possible (cf. *Inter insigniores* by Pope John Paul II) (*Catechism*, 1577).

Chapter 19

THE VOCATION OF THE LAITY

The active presence of the laity in the work of the church is most evident in Catholic schools, colleges, hospitals and religious education programs. Their active ministry is equally seen at liturgy in their roles as lectors, eucharistic ministers, hospitality ministers, choir members, ushers and members of parish councils and committees.

By reason of their special vocation it belongs to the laity to seek the kingdom of God by engaging in temporal affairs and directing them according to God's will ... It pertains to them in a special way so to illuminate and order all temporal things with which they are closely associated that these may always be effected and grow according to Christ and may be to the glory of the Creator and Redeemer (*Catechism, 898*).

The laity are on the front line of the church's life. It is precisely through the laity that the church is, practically speaking, a source of moral and spiritual life for society. Lay people should have "an ever-clearer consciousness not only of belonging to the Church, but of being the Church, that is to say, the community of the faithful on earth under the leadership of the Pope, the common Head, and of the bishops in communion with him. They are the Church" (*Catechism, 899*).

The Vocation of the Laity

■ **A. What is the laity's participation in Christ's priestly office?**
All their works, prayers, and apostolic undertakings, family and married life, daily work, relaxation of mind and body, if they are accomplished in the Spirit—indeed even the hardships of life if patiently borne—all these become spiritual sacrifices acceptable to God through Jesus Christ. In the celebration of the Eucharist these may most fittingly be offered to the Father along with the body of the Lord. In a very special way, parents share in the office of sanctifying "by leading a conjugal life in the Christian spirit and by seeing to the Christian education of their children" (*Catechism, 901-902*).

■ **B. Describe the laity's prophetic call.**
Lay people also fulfill their prophetic mission by evangelization, "that is, the proclamation of Christ by word and the testimony of life." For lay people, "this evangelization ... acquires a specific property and peculiar efficacy because it is accomplished in the ordinary circumstances of the world" (*Catechism, 905*).

■ **C. What is the laity's kingly vocation?**
That man is rightly called a king who makes his own body an obedient subject and, by governing himself with suitable rigor, refuses to let his passions breed rebellion in his soul, for he exercises a kind of royal power over himself. And because he knows how to rule his own person as king, so too does he sit as its judge. He will not let himself be imprisoned by sin, or thrown headlong into wickedness (St. Ambrose, *On Psalm 118:14, 30*) (*Catechism, 908*).

1 **What is meant by the term "laity"?**

The term "laity" is here understood to mean all the faithful except those in Holy Orders and those who belong to a religious state approved by the Church. That is, the faithful, who by Baptism are incorporated into Christ and integrated into the People of God, are made sharers in their particular way in the priestly, prophetic, and kingly office of Christ, and have their own part to play in the mission of the whole Christian people in the Church and in the world (*Catechism, 897*).

> *Lay people should have an ever-clearer consciousness not only of belonging to the church, but of being the church.*

2 What is meant by the word "ministry"?

Ministry means to give service. In this context it means to share in carrying out the mission and service of Jesus Christ, who said "... I must proclaim the good news of the kingdom of God ... for I was sent for this purpose" (Lk 4:43). Whenever we have the opportunity to spread Jesus' good news through words, actions or spirit, we are called to ministry.

In its most general use, ministry can refer to the way we live our lives in light of our baptism. More specifically, it refers to areas of work such as health care, youth work or serving as special ministers of the Eucharist who assist the priest at Mass. Finally, the word identifies those called to ordained ministry in the sacrament of holy orders—that is deacons, priests and bishops.

3 Can lay people minister in the church?

The sacrament of baptism introduces a person into the common priesthood, described by St. Peter as ". . . a royal priesthood, God's own people, in order that you may proclaim the mighty acts of him" (1 Pt 2:9).

No ministry in the church is more needed and enduring than that which proclaims God's glorious works. Peter tells all baptized people that God commissioned them to this ministry. Therefore, every lay person has the vocation to be a minister of Christ in the church.

4 What is the relationship between the ordained and the laity in ministry?

Baptism calls people to ministry. In holy orders, however, certain people are commissioned to do specific works, such as preaching and celebrating the Eucharist and the rite of reconciliation. In addition, ordained bishops and priests are to be the leaders of dioceses and parishes.

Laity and ordained persons should work together in a collaborative and complementary manner, to build the Body of Christ through evangelization, liturgical celebrations and services of love, justice and mercy. All members are participating in the mission of Jesus.

5 In what kinds of ministry can lay people participate?

People can participate in several levels of ministry in the church. Included in those levels are *formal* ministries, those in the *marketplace* and ministry in the *home*.

6 What are *formal* ministries, and how can lay people participate in them?

Formal ministries are those roles which pertain to carrying out the work of the church. For this reason, administrative positions in religious education and pastoral ministry are filled by qualified lay people. Although some positions require a full time commitment, others may be filled on a volunteer basis. For example, lay positions on parish councils and finance committees are formal ministries within the church.

7 What is meant by ministry *in the marketplace*?

Pope Paul VI explained the unique ministry of lay people as being that which encompasses "... the wide and complex arena of politics, sociology and economics ... the spheres of culture, the sciences, the arts, international relations and the communications media."

The Holy Father continued, "If laymen who are actively involved in these spheres are inspired with the evangelical spirit, if they are competent and determined to bring into play all those Christian powers in themselves which so often lie hidden and dormant, then all these activities will be all the more helpful in the building up of the kingdom of God and in bringing salvation in Jesus Christ" (*Evangelization*, 70).

8 What is meant by ministry *in the home*?

"... the family in the sphere of the apostolate which is proper to the laity. It has rightly been called the *domestic* church and this title has been confirmed by the second Vatican council. It declares that in every Christian family the various features and characteristics of the universal church should be found. And accordingly, the family, just like the church, must always be regarded as a center to which the gospel must be brought and from which it must be proclaimed" (*Evangelization*, 71).

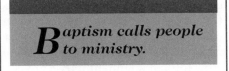

Baptism calls people to ministry.

Therefore, being a good parent, a good spouse or a helpful family member *is ministry*. As such, we announce the good news of the reign of God in a concrete manner. This is not only true when we are specifically *talking* about God or praying together. We are ministering whenever we engage in activities which build our family as a happy, loving community, which is consciously living a Christian life.

9 Does this mean that all our actions are ministry?

No, it does not. Ministry is "... the work that is done by those who believe in Jesus in service to each other and the world around them, that members of the Christian community perform in the name of Christ" (*Origins*, Vol. 5, No. 34).

Just about every activity has the potential to be ministry. When we are motivated by our baptism, living every day as Jesus did, and acting in his name, we are proclaiming his kingdom. That is ministry.

10 Why have the activities of lay people increased so greatly within the church?

Since Vatican II, there has been a tremendous increase in theological support for lay involvement in the church. At the same time, a decline in the number of clergy has made it both necessary and possible for the laity to join the various ministries of the church. Therefore, the presence of lay men and women as lectors and eucharistic ministers, for example, is part of a fresh vision of lay participation in the church.

11 Have lay people always been encouraged to participate in ministries?

Catholics have always been encouraged to use their gifts in service to others. Although the word ministry was not used for these works in the past, lay people have been challenged to do spiritual and corporal works of mercy.

The expanded role of the laity was highlighted in the writings of twentieth-century popes. Pope Pius X spoke of the laity as a *flock* whose primary responsibility is to allow itself to be led; Pius XI encouraged participation in the *apostolate of the hierarchy*; and Pius XII encouraged lay people to explore their own calling to the church's *Mystical Body*.

Terms such as *lay apostolate* and *Catholic action* were popular around the time of Vatican II. The use of these terms in documents like Pope Paul VI's *On Evangelization in the Modern World* helped make their use widespread, and the concept of lay ministry more versatile.

12 How should Catholics minister?

In the broadest sense, ministry is *service*. Every Catholic should serve his or her family, church and all others with justice, love and mercy. After Jesus washed the feet of his apostles on Holy Thursday night, he told them, "For I have set you an example, that you also should do as I have done to you" (Jn 13:15).

Jesus' actions, therefore, serve as examples for us in forming our relationships with others. In addition, Catholics should participate, wherever possible, in the church's many special ministries, either as ordained or lay community members.

13 What training do lay people need for ministry?

The basic level of training for ministry is a good formation in the Christian way of life. Developing an adult understanding and experience of faith allows mature Catholics to share their faith. Knowing Jesus as *friend* and *Lord* is the basic motivation for ministry.

Some specific skills are needed, however, for special ministries. For example, lectors must have public speaking training, understand the flow of liturgy and must possess special respect and love for Scripture. In addition to their faith and understanding, religious education teachers must have

> *We are ministering whenever we engage in activities that build our family as a happy, loving community.*

classroom skills and knowledge of childhood development.

14 How do lay people obtain the necessary skills for ministry?

Training resources are usually available through local parishes or diocesan education programs. Often, program participants are granted certification indicating their fitness to work in specific ministries.

Professional-level ministries often require specialized training and education. For this work, lay people may attend classes given at Catholic colleges or seminaries.

15 What is the call to holiness that makes lay ministry so effective?

"It is evident to everyone that all the faithful of Christ of whatever rank or status are called to the fullness of the Christian life and to the perfection of charity. By this holiness a more human way of life is promoted even in this earthly society. In order that the faithful may reach this perfection, they must use their strength according as they have received it, as a gift from Christ ... In this way too, the holiness of the People of God will grow into an abundant harvest of good, as is brilliantly proved by the lives of so many saints in Church history" (*Church*, 40).

"All of Christ's faithful, therefore, whatever be the conditions, duties, and circumstances of their lives, will grow in holiness day by day through these very situations, if they accept all of them with faith from the hand of their heavenly Father, and if they cooperate with the divine will by showing every man through their earthly activities the love with which God has loved the world" (*Church*, 41).

SOCIAL JUSTICE

Chapter
20

Every night, even in this most modern of centuries, millions of people go to bed hungry. Countless numbers of these are children suffering from malnutrition. Here at home, inner city blacks and Hispanics argue that the richest country in the world treats them as "second class citizens." They properly cry out for respect, dignity and social justice.

"Social justice can be obtained only in respecting the transcendent dignity of man. The person represents the ultimate end of society, which is ordered to him: 'What is at stake is the dignity of the human person, whose defense and promotion have been entrusted to us by the Creator, and to whom the men and women at every moment of history are strictly and responsibly in debt'" (Pope John Paul II, *SRS* 47) (*Catechism*, 1929).

"Society ensures social justice when it provides the conditions that allow associations or individuals to obtain what is their due, according to their nature and their vocation. Social justice is linked to the common good and the exercise of authority" (*Catechism*, 1928).

Social Justice

■ A. What is the basis for respecting human dignity?
Respect for the human person entails respect for the rights that flow from his dignity as a creature. These rights are prior to society and must be recognized by it. They are the basis of the moral legitimacy of every authority: by flouting them, or refusing to recognize them in its positive legislation, a society undermines its own moral legitimacy. If it does not respect them, authority can rely only on force or violence to obtain obedience from its subjects. It is the Church's role to remind men of good will of these rights, and to distinguish them from unwarranted or false claims (*Catechism*, 1930).

■ B. Are all people equal?
Created in the image of the one God and equally endowed with rational souls, all men have the same nature and the same origin. Redeemed by the sacrifice of Christ, all are called to participate in the same divine beatitude: all therefore enjoy an equal dignity. "Every form of social or cultural discrimination in fundamental personal rights on the grounds of sex, race, color, social conditions, language, or religion must be curbed and eradicated as incompatible with God's design" (*Church*, 29) (*Catechism*, 1934-1935).

■ C. How is human solidarity expressed?
The principle of solidarity, also articulated in terms of "friendship" or "social charity," is a direct demand of human and Christian brotherhood. "An error, 'today abundantly widespread, is disregard for the law of human solidarity and charity, dictated and imposed both by our common origin and by the equality in rational nature of all men, whatever nation they belong to. This law is sealed by the sacrifice of redemption offered by Jesus Christ on the altar of the Cross to his heavenly Father, on behalf of sinful humanity'" (Pope Pius XII, *Summi pontificatus*) (*Catechism*, 1939).

1 **What story in the Old Testament teaches us the most about justice?**

The *supreme* experience of the people of God in the Old Testament was their liberation from unjust oppression in Egypt. From their slave labor camps they sent a cry to heaven for liberation. God heard their pleas and raised up Moses to be their liberator.

The Jews viewed their political deliverance from an unjust social situation as an act of divine salvation. Thereafter, they celebrated their Exodus from Egypt as the *greatest* moment of justice in their history. They praised God who loved them so much that he gave them the justice they fervently sought.

2 Did the Old Testament people of God uphold the ideals of justice in their society?

Jewish laws reflected the practices of love, justice and mercy. Their statutes called for care and concern for orphans, widows, debtors and the enslaved (Dt 10:17 ff.; 15:11). However, they were prone to human weakness and sin. Thanks to their openness to the grace of God, prophets arose to stir up the people's consciences and embrace God's ideals of justice.

3 What did the prophet Amos teach the Hebrew people about justice?

Amos was the first of the great reforming prophets (750 BC). He was horrified by the people's departure from the simplest standards of decency. He was shocked by the luxury and self-indulgence of the rich, who slept on beds of ivory, while treating the poor shamelessly and ignoring their basic needs (Am 6).

His short, social ministry gave the world one of the first documents of social protest. Amos proclaimed an ethical God who was affronted by worshippers who used religion to *mask* and justify immorality. He scourged his people because he loved them and wept over them because they loved neither God nor people.

4 How does Jesus teach the need for justice?

When Jesus proclaims the kingdom, he speaks of a salvation from sin and injustice (Lk 4:14-21). In his Sermon on the Mount, Last Supper Discourse and attacks on hypocritical Pharisees, he carried forward the teachings of the prophets on justice.

His parables of the Good Samaritan and the Rich Man and Lazarus are eloquent pleas for concern and justice. In his healing miracles, Christ acted out his position on justice and mercy. In his own fair treatment of others Jesus showed us the importance of moral conscience in human behavior.

5 Are there other New Testament teachings about justice?

The New Testament teaches that all human beings are brothers and sisters under God, whom they call "Our Father in heaven" (Mt 6:9). Everyone is equal before God. "There is no longer Jew or Greek, there is no longer slave or free, there is no longer male and female; for all of you are one in Christ Jesus" (Gal 3:28). "For he (Christ) is our peace" (Eph 2:14).

6 What is the departure point for Catholic social teaching?

Catholic social teaching begins with affirming the sacredness and dignity of the human person. The church teaches that we are human beings from the moment of conception, created by God in his

> *Catholic social teaching begins with affirming the sacredness and dignity of the human person.*

image (Gn 1:26) and destined to be with him forever. The psalmist and the writers of the New Testament state many times that human beings are the pinnacle of God's visible creation.

"All things are of your making, all times and seasons obey your laws, but you chose to create man in your own image, setting him over the whole world in all its wonder" (*Preface V for Sundays in Ordinary Time*).

7 What is an immediate consequence of the dignity of the human person?

Human dignity involves the stewardship of all creation. Human beings are to cooperate with the Creator in fulfilling the potential of creation. Men and women also are to see that the social, technical and economic aspects of creation are to be put to the service of human beings.

Further, men and women are to see that the spiritual, psychological, emotional and bodily integrity of the human person is respected as a fundamental value.

8 How do "rights" and "duties" fit into this vision of human dignity?

A correct understanding of human dignity generates an appreciation of the human rights and duties that attend the sacredness of human persons. As human beings we have basic rights and duties, regardless of our level of intelligence, background, contribution to society, race, sex or vocation.

For us, rights and duties are complementary. When one person has a right, others have a duty to respect that right. Pope John XXIII listed a catalogue of basic human rights in his encyclical *Peace on Earth.*

9 What is the importance of seeing a human being as a social being?

Because all humans are social by nature, the family, society and the state are natural environments for human living. Social structures are essential for personal development at all levels, including the religious level.

We must remember to pay close attention to those elements that affect the social order—laws, forms of government, financial and economic systems and cultural expectations. Each of these structures involves moral standards that affect human beings.

10 What is the purpose of Catholic social teaching?

Catholic social teaching helps the church and her members to develop principles to evaluate how well social structures minister to the good of the individual and the common good. The church's moral and spiritual guidelines for *personal behavior* are complemented by the same guidelines for judging and evaluating *social structures.*

11 How should we relate personal and social morality?

It should be clear to us that personal and social morality are distinct realities. They are not, however, separate, nor should they be too sharply divided. The word of God and the Lord's moral imperative stand in judgment on all personal deeds and social institutions. Because of the complexity of social issues, their *moral* correctness requires astute probing.

Pope Paul VI stated that "It is difficult for us to utter a unified message and to put forth a solution that has universal validity ... It is up to the Christian communities to analyze with objectivity the situation which is proper to their own country, to shed on it the light of God's unalterable words and to draw principles of reflection, norms of judgment and directives for action from the social teachings of the church."

12 Does the Catholic Church see itself as having a social mission?

For most of its history the church has been engaged in the corporal works of mercy (cf. Mt 25:31-40). These constitute an essential part of Christian moral behavior.

> **B**oth the church as an institution and we as members are called to action on behalf of justice.

During the last one hundred years, the church has been working on a systematic development of moral teaching on social issues. In recent years, the church is taking up the question of her mission in matters of justice. It is studying the development of a social ministry intrinsically related to the church's role. This move emerges in her *Dogmatic Constitution on the Church* and in the *Pastoral Constitution on the Church in the Modern World.*

13 Is the question of the church's social ministry addressed in other documents?

One reads in the introduction to *Justice in the World* that "Action on behalf of justice and participation in the transformation of the world appear to us as a constitutive dimension of the preaching of the gospel; or in other words, of the Church's mission for the redemption of the human race, and its liberation from every oppressive situation."

Pope Paul VI said, "While recognizing the connection between them, the Church never identifies human liberation with salvation in Jesus Christ" (*Evangelization*, 35). In other words, salvation refers to being delivered from sin. Human liberation speaks of deliverance from injustice, which is a living out of our salvation. On the occasion of the *Call to Action* meeting, Pope Paul VI pointed out that "The cause of human dignity and of human rights is the cause of Christ and his gospel."

14 How does the church's social mission affect our call to this ministry?

Both the church as an institution and we as members are called to action on behalf of justice. This should not be the work of a few in the church. Rather, each of us should dedicate ourselves to the cause of justice.

A significant priority in the work of justice is a preferential option for the poor. This does not imply an exclusion of anyone in need, but it does call for a preference to help the oppressed and victimized.

15 What are the church documents that refer to social conscience and behavior?

Some key papal encyclicals on social issues are *Rerum Novarum (On the Condition of Labor,* Leo XIII, 1891); *Quadragesimo Anno* (On the Fortieth Anniversary of *Rerum Novarum,* Pius XI, 1931*); Mater et Magistra (Mother and Teacher,* John XXIII, 1961); *Pacem in Terris (Peace on Earth,* John XXIII, 1963); *Populorum Progressio (On the Development of Peoples,* Paul VI, 1967); *Octogesima Adveniens (A Call to Action,* Paul VI, 1971); and *Redemptor Hominis (Man's Redeemer,* John Paul II, 1979).

The document *Justice in the World* resulted from the 1971 Synod on Justice. Social issues are also addressed in the documents of the Second Vatican Council.

16 What are some of the rules that guide us as Christians?

Christ calls us all to be good samaritans and prophets. As good samaritans, Christians minister to the individual needs of the deprived and disadvantaged. We should feed the hungry, clothe the naked, visit the sick and console the despairing and those who mourn.

> *Christ calls us all to be good samaritans and prophets.*

The good samaritan engages in personal acts of love and mercy and helps to heal the symptoms of injustice. Such is the calling of Mother Teresa of India or of St. Vincent de Paul. To care for the symptoms of injustice is a most Christian work. The church shall always need good samaritans.

As prophets we are called to take action to heal the causes of injustice. This requires action that helps reform those aspects of society that are oppressing the poor. Labor unions grew out of such a concern, as did the civil rights movement. These acts sought to remove the causes of injustice to the worker and to those who are black.

For over a century now, the popes and many others within the church have been striving to awaken the prophetic vocation of all Christians—a vocation to heal the causes of injustice.

"THAT THEY MAY ALL BE ONE"
(JOHN 17:21)

"What an astonishing mystery! There is one Father of the universe, one *Logos* of the universe and also one Holy Spirit, everywhere one and the same. There is also one virgin become mother, and I should like to call her Church" (St. Clement of Alexandria, *Paed*, 1, 6,42).

Unity is an essential mark of the church. The church is one because her source is the unity of persons in the Trinity. She is one because of her founder, Jesus Christ, who has reconciled the world to the Father and has restored the unity of all people in one body.

But for a variety of historical, political and economic reasons—including human sinfulness—the church has split apart over the centuries into many denominations. Vatican II called the Catholic Church to enter into dialogue with all Christian denominations for the purpose of recovering the unity that Jesus prayed for at the Last Supper: "That they may all be one. As you, Father, are in me and I am in you" (Jn 17:21).

The result of this call has been the ecumenical movement and the processes of dialogue between the Catholic Church and other communions such as the Orthodox, Anglican, Lutheran, Methodist and Presbyterian churches.

"That they may all be one" (*John 17:21*).

■ A. What must we do to achieve Church unity?
Certain things are required in order to respond adequately to this call:

- a permanent *renewal* of the Church in greater fidelity to her vocation; such renewal is the driving-force of the movement toward unity;
- *conversion of heart* as the faithful "try to live holier lives according to the Gospel"; for it is the unfaithfulness of the members to Christ's gift which causes divisions;

- *prayer in common*, because "change of heart and holiness of life, along with public and private prayer for the unity of Christians, should be regarded as the soul of the whole ecumenical movement, and merits the name 'spiritual ecumenism'";
- *fraternal knowledge of each other*;
- *ecumenical formation* of the faithful and especially of priests;
- *dialogue* among theologians and meetings among Christians of the different churches and communities;
- *collaboration* among Christians in various areas of service to mankind. "Human service" is the idiomatic phrase (*Catechism*, 821).

■ B. Are divisions in Christianity new?
"In this one and only Church of God from its very beginnings there arose certain rifts, which the Apostle strongly censures as damnable. But in subsequent centuries much more serious dissensions appeared and large communities became separated from full communion with the Catholic Church—for which, often enough, men of both sides were to blame" (*Ecumenism*, 3). The ruptures that wound the unity of Christ's Body—here we must distinguish heresy, apostasy, and schism—do not occur without human sin (*Catechism*, 817).

■ C. Does Christ's saving grace work in other Christian churches?
Christ's Spirit uses these Churches and ecclesial communities as means of salvation, whose power derives from the fullness of grace and truth that Christ has entrusted to the Catholic Church. All these blessings come from Christ and lead to him, and are in themselves calls to "Catholic unity" (*Catechism*, 819).

81

1 Why is there disunity among the Christian churches?

The reasons for the split in Christianity are much like the reasons for disunity among people. The causes include misunderstanding, sinfulness,

> *T*he diversity of rites is seen as a positive value.

shortsightedness, impatience and pride and sluggishness on the part of church leaders.

Historically, political opportunism among royalty created exploitation of religious differences for their own military and economic gains. In addition, cultural changes caused breakdowns in communications and the consequent failure to resolve conflicts.

2 What are the major splits Christianity has experienced?

In the eleventh century the churches of Eastern Europe and the Middle East broke with Rome. They refused to accept the authority of the pope and became known as Orthodox churches. This event is called the Eastern Schism.

The Protestant Reformation took place in the sixteenth century. It created new churches in Germany, Switzerland, England, Scotland, Holland and Scandinavia, and eventually in the United States.

3 What is schism?

"*Schism* is the refusal of submission to the Roman Pontiff or of communion with the members of the Church subject to him" (*Catechism*, 2089).

4 What do Orthodox churches have in common with the Catholic Church?

Orthodox and Catholic Christians have the same basic teachings, moral position (for the most part), Eucharist, sacraments and devotion to Mary and the saints. They also have bishops, priests, deacons, monks and nuns. In addition, they share a profound sense of the mystery and awesomeness of God. They reflect a special *reverence* for Scripture and the work of the Holy Spirit.

5 What are the Eastern Rite churches?

They are those Eastern Churches which are united with Rome. For this reason they are often called "Uniate Churches," which means *in union with* Rome. Although they are different from Latin (Roman) Rite churches, they are members of the Catholic Church.

"The liturgical traditions or rites presently in use in the Church are the Latin ... and the Byzantine, Alexandrian or Coptic, Syriac, Armenian, Maronite, and Chaldean rites. 'In faithful obedience to tradition, the sacred Council declares that Holy Mother Church holds all lawfully recognized rites to be of equal right and dignity, and that she wishes to preserve them in the future and to foster them in every way'" (*Catechism*, 1203).

6 How do the rites of the Eastern Church differ from those of the Latin Church?

The use of the word *rite* goes far beyond the specific rituals for liturgies. It refers to a point of view on theology, prayer, spirituality, church discipline and ritual expression. Just as there is a western cultural outlook in the Latin Rite, there are cultural perspectives in the Greek, Maronite, Armenian, Russian and Melkite rites.

7 Does this diversity of rites impede the unity of the church?

No, diversity does not impede the unity of the church. There is still one Lord, one faith, one baptism and one church amid these profound cultural expressions. Eastern Rite churches reflect development and a tradition that goes back to New Testament times.

8 How did the Vatican Council view the diversity of rites?

The diversity of rites is seen as a positive value. "... The Mystical Body of Christ is made up of the faithful who are organically united in the Holy Spirit through the same faith, the same sacraments, and the same government and who, combining into various groups held together by a hierarchy, form separate Churches or rites. Between these, there flourishes such an admirable brotherhood that this variety within the Church in no way harms her unity, ... it is the mind of the Catholic Church that each individual Church or rite retain its traditions whole and entire, while adjusting its way of life to the various needs of time and place" (*Decree on Eastern Catholic Churches*, 2).

9 What is the meaning of *ecumenism*?

Ecumenism is the term referring to the dialogue existing between Catholic, Orthodox and Protestant churches with the goal of seeking Christian unity. The spirit of this movement flows from the desire of Christ expressed at the Last Supper. "I ask ... that they may all be one. As you, Father, are in me, and I am in you ... that the world may believe that you have sent me" (Jn 17:20,21).

10 How does the Catholic Church view the Orthodox churches?

The Catholic Church feels a special bond with those Eastern churches which are not in full communion with it. This is because these churches "... possess true sacraments, above all—by apostolic succession—the priesthood and the Eucharist ... this entire heritage of spirituality and liturgy, of discipline and theology, in their various traditions, belongs to the full catholic and apostolic character of the Church" (*Decree on Ecumenism*, 15, 17).

11 How does the Catholic Church view Protestant churches?

The Catholic Church recognizes the separate churches and ecclesial communities of the West in a very positive way. It has a special affinity and close relationship with them, arising from the long span of earlier centuries when Christians lived in ecclesiastical communion.

Several of the churches have maintained Catholic traditions and institutions and have a close relationship with the Catholic Church (cf. *Sharing the Light of Faith*, 75) .

12 To what extent is the Catholic Church involved in ecumenism?

The church is actively involved in the ecumenical movement. It has established a Secretariat for Christian Unity at the Vatican. In addition, it cosponsors developments such as the Anglican-Catholic Dialogue, Lutheran-Catholic Dialogue and the Orthodox-Catholic Dialogue.

13 Are there any rules for ecumenical sensitivity among Catholics?

The following could be considered rules for ecumenical sensitivity among Catholics:
■ a) Work for the renewal of the church and its members;
■ b) Present Catholic teaching in a straightforward and complete way;
■ c) Explain the positions of other Christian churches in a fair and honest manner, free of prejudice and bias;
■ d) While stressing where we differ, also highlight where we agree in doctrine and shared values; and
■ e) Promote cooperation in projects for the common good.

14 Why does the church seek dialogue with non-Christian religions?

Just as the church seeks the unity of all Christians, she also believes she should promote unity and love among all people. God is the single origin of all people. At the same time he is our *ultimate* goal.

The church accepts the responsibility of helping all people reach unity with God on earth and union with him hereafter.

15 What is the church's attitude toward religions such as Hinduism and Buddhism?

"The Catholic Church rejects nothing which is true and holy in these religions. She looks with sincere respect upon those ways of conduct and of life, those rules and teachings which, though dif-

> *Just as the church seeks the unity of all Christians, she also believes she should promote unity and love among all people.*

fering in many particulars from what she holds and sets forth, nevertheless often reflect a ray of that Truth which enlightens all men" (*Declaration on the Relationship of the Church to Non-Christian Religions*, 2).

The church encourages dialogue and cooperation with the members of these religions. She asks us to do this with prudence and love, always witnessing Christian faith and life. The church calls us to recognize, preserve and promote the positive spiritual, moral and socio-cultural values found among the members of these religions.

16 What is the viewpoint of the church on the Moslem religion?

The church has high esteem for the Moslem religion. Moslems worship the living God and believe in him in the same manner as Abraham, with whom they link themselves. They revere Jesus as a prophet, though not as God. In addition, Moslems honor Mary and value a moral and spiritual life.

Unfortunately, violence and hatred marked the relationship of the church and Moslems in centuries past. The church today asks that Christians and Moslems work together for mutual understanding to bring about justice and peace (cf. *Non-Christian Religions*, 3).

17 What are some of the spiritual links between the church and Judaism?

The following are included among the spiritual links between the church and Judaism:
■ a) The divine plan of salvation began with Abraham and continued through the patriarchs and prophets. For Christians, this plan was then fulfilled in Christ.
■ b) The church's salvation is mysteriously foreshadowed in the Exodus salvation of the Hebrew people.

■ c) The church received the Hebrew Scriptures from a people with whom God established a covenant at Sinai.

The church keeps in mind the words of Paul: "To them belong the adoption, the glory, the covenants, the giving of the law, the worship, and the promises; to them belong the patriarchs, and from them, according to the flesh, comes the Messiah, who is over all, God blessed forever. Amen" (Rom 9:4,5).

"Since the spiritual patrimony common to Christians and Jews is thus so great, this sacred Synod wishes to foster and recommend that mutual understanding and respect which is the fruit above all of biblical and theological studies, and of brotherly dialogues" (*Non-Christian Religions*, 4).

18 What does the church say about anti-Semitism?

The church rejects anti-Semitism. It also rejects the false religious premise from which it arises, namely that all Jews are responsible for the death of Christ. "True, authorities of the Jews and those who followed their lead pressed for the death of

> *The church rejects anti-Semitism.*

Christ; still, what happened in His passion cannot be blamed upon all the Jews then living, without distinction, nor upon the Jews of today. Although the Church is the new people of God, the Jews should not be presented as repudiated or cursed by God, as if such views followed from the holy Scriptures" (*Non-Christian Religions*, 4).

HOLY MARY, MOTHER OF GOD, PRAY FOR US

Novelist Nathaniel Hawthorne once wrote, "I have always envied Catholics that sweet, sacred Virgin Mother, who stands between them and the Deity. She intercepts (somewhat) his awesome splendor."

Mary and the saints lend a touch of nearness to God, who otherwise might seem too far out of our reach. The saints open further means of contact, just as Jesus gave us human access to the Father.

The greatness of Mary and the saints arises from their exemplary earthly lives and their close union with Jesus, their obedience of faith to the Father's will under the guidance of the Holy Spirit. Writer George Bernard Shaw once confided that he found it difficult to believe in God, but he was hopeful that "his Mother will see me through."

When we visit Mary, we are immediately turned over to Jesus. We are reminded that at the Visitation, Christ's presence filled Elizabeth with joy, causing St. John to leap in her womb. There is joy in knowing Jesus through Mary and the saints.

Holy Mary, Mother of God, Pray for Us

■ A. How is the greatness of Mary seen at the Annunciation?

At the announcement that she would give birth to "the Son of the Most High" without knowing man, by the power of the Holy Spirit, Mary responded with the obedience of faith, certain that "with God nothing will be impossible": "Behold, I am the handmaid of the Lord; let it be [done] to me according to your word" (*Lk* 1:28-38). Thus, giving her consent to God's Word, Mary becomes the mother of Jesus. Espousing the divine will for salvation wholeheartedly, without a single sin to restrain her, she gave herself entirely to the person and to the work of her Son; she did so in order to serve the mystery of

redemption with him and dependent on him, by God's grace (*Catechism*, 494).

■ B. How closely is Mary linked to the mystery of the church?

Mary's role in the Church is inseparable from her union with Christ and flows directly from it. "This union of the mother with the Son in the work of salvation is made manifest from the time of Christ's virginal conception up to his death" (*Church*, 57). After her Son's Ascension, Mary "aided the beginnings of the Church by her prayers." In her association with the apostles and several women, "we also see Mary by her prayers imploring the gift of the Spirit, who had already overshadowed her in the Annunciation" (*Church*, 59) (*Catechism*, 964-965).

■ C. Why do we ask Mary to pray for us?

This motherhood of Mary in the order of grace continues uninterruptedly from the consent which she loyally gave at the Annunciation and which she sustained without wavering beneath the cross, until the eternal fulfillment of all the elect. Taken up to heaven she did not lay aside this saving office but by her manifold intercession continues to bring us the gifts of eternal salvation ... Therefore the Blessed Virgin is invoked in the Church under the titles of Advocate, Helper, Benefactress, and Mediatrix" (*Church*, 62) (*Catechism*, 969).

1 Is someone like Mary foreshadowed in the Old Testament?

The Old Testament does not specifically speak of Mary, but it does recite events that form a unity, purpose and pattern. The life of Mary is part of that *pattern* of salvation history. This history is not seen as a series of disconnected events. The people of faith discern a pattern, a plan, a unity in the entire experience, from creation to redemption and the end of the world. Mary reflects and brings fuller meaning to events that preceded her.

Church tradition teaches that Mary, the virgin who will give birth to the Messiah, is foreshadowed in several Scripture references. For example, we learn in the Old Testament that a woman will give

> **M**ary and the saints lend a touch of nearness to God.

birth to a savior from evil: "I will put enmity between you and the woman, and between your offspring and hers ..." (Gn 3:15).

Also, we see in Isaiah the prophecy that a virgin will give birth to a messiah. "Therefore the Lord himself will give you a sign. Look, the young woman is with child and shall bear a son, and shall name him Immanuel" (Is 7:14).

Church tradition sees in the ark of the covenant a symbol of Mary. Just as the ark "carried" the presence of God, so did Mary carry the Son of God in her womb.

2 Why is Mary's consent to be the mother of God important?

At the Annunciation, the angel Gabriel asked Mary to be the mother of God's Son. She surrendered to the call, saying, "Here am I, the servant of the Lord; let it be with me according to your word" (Lk 1:38).

Again, in her song of joy, the *Magnificat*, Mary declared that "The Mighty One has done great things for me" (Lk 1:49).

Mary's consent is important because she sums up personally and collectively the faith of the good people of Israel who are obedient to God. In addition, her consent helps set in motion, historically, the salvation of the world.

3 How is Mary's relationship to Jesus' ministry portrayed in the Gospels?

In Mark's Gospel, Jesus speaks of his mother who practices the obedience of faith. "Who are my mother and my brothers? ... Whoever does the will of God is my brother and sister and mother" (Mk 3:33, 35). In Luke (8:21) and Matthew (12:50) we see this theme repeated.

John's Gospel illustrates her faith in action. At the feast of Cana, Mary calls Jesus to begin his active ministry. The scene concludes with these words: "Jesus did this, the first of his signs, in Cana of Galilee, and revealed his glory ..." (Jn 2:11).

John further shows Mary as loyal mother and woman of faith at the foot of the cross. Jesus calls her to be the mother of the church: "Woman, here is your son" (Jn 19:26). The New Testament story of her faith life is crowned by her presence at Pentecost. Here, she stood as the principal witness of faith and woman of prayer among the believers in the upper room, awaiting the coming of the Spirit (Acts 1:14).

4 Is Mary the *woman* spoken of in the Book of Revelation?

Revelation tells us that "A great portent appeared in heaven: a woman clothed with the sun ... gave birth to a son ..." (12:1,5). Later, a dragon appeared and goes on to "... make war on the rest of her children, those who keep the commandments of God and hold the testimony of Jesus" (v. 17).

Some biblical interpreters see the woman as Israel giving birth to the Messiah and the church which gives birth to Christians. Many others see the woman as Mary giving birth to both Jesus and Christianity.

There seem to be enough persuasive arguments to favor the woman as symbolizing both the church and Mary. The Fathers of the church see Mary as the symbol of a Mother Church that begets Christians.

5 Was Mary always a virgin?

The Catholic Church holds it as a matter of faith that Mary was always a virgin. The Apostles' Creed and the Nicene Creed affirm that Jesus was "born of the virgin Mary." "The deepening of faith in the virginal motherhood led the Church to confess Mary's real and perpetual virginity even in the act of giving birth to the Son of God made man ... The liturgy of the Church celebrates Mary as *Aeiparthenos,* the 'Ever-Virgin'" (*Church*, 52) (*Catechism*, 499).

6 What is the religious significance of Mary's virginity?

Speaking of Mary's virginity, the church addresses the uniqueness of Jesus, and that he comes from God. Her virginity also signifies that, in Christ, the human race has a *new beginning*.

The message of Mary's virginity also tells us that God works through human agents—often the weak, the humble and the poor.

7 What did the Council of Ephesus say about Mary?

Christians in the fourth and fifth centuries devoted considerable attention to the question of Jesus' divinity and humanity. They struggled with the issue of how the two natures were united in Jesus and sought to protect his full humanity and divinity and the unity between these two elements.

At the Council of Ephesus (held in 431), the church Fathers rejected the teaching of Nestorius, which stated there were two persons in Jesus: one human and the other divine. Instead, the council resolved that there is a divine and human nature in Christ, but only one *divine person*. We find God, they said, in the *man* Jesus.

In order to reinforce this teaching, the council bestowed upon Mary the title of *Theotokos* (in Greek, the God carrier) or the Mother of God.

8 What is the meaning of Mary's "Immaculate Conception"?

On December 8, 1854, Pope Pius IX declared "That the Blessed Virgin Mary was, from the first moment of her conception, by the singular grace and privilege of almighty God, and in view of the merits of Jesus Christ, preserved immune from all stain of original sin."

We find the rationale for this in the opening prayer for the Immaculate Conception feast. "Father, you prepared the Virgin Mary to be the worthy mother of your Son. You let her share beforehand in the salvation Jesus would bring by his death and kept her sinless from the first moment of her conception."

9 What is the meaning of the Assumption of the Virgin Mary?

In 1950 Pope Pius XII declared the dogma of Mary's Assumption. In doing so, he said, "It was her crowning glory to be preserved from the corruption of the tomb, and like her Son before her, to conquer death and be raised body and soul to the glory of heaven."

The opening prayer for the memorial of Mary's Assumption, celebrated each August 15, states, "All powerful and ever living God, you raised the sinless virgin Mary, Mother of your Son, body and soul to the glory of heaven. May we see heaven as our final goal and come to share her glory."

10 How does Mary affect our lives as Christians?

First, Mary is a *symbol* of the church. Just as she gave birth to Jesus, so does the church give birth to Christians in the baptismal font. At the same time, Mary is our spiritual mother, called by Jesus to do this when at the cross he said to her, "Woman, here is your son."

Second, Mary is a *model* for Christian believers. She was the first and greatest Christian. She

> *Mary prays for us as our loving Mother and fellow Christian.*

has been a luminous model of faith, hope and love. Her "yes" at the Annunciation was the beginning of a lifelong surrender to the will of God.

There is no other believer in Jesus who has been honored more than Mary in the history of the church. Nowhere can one find a greater example of strong Christian behavior. For this reason, Mary has been forcefully upheld as a model for each of us.

Third, Mary *prays* for us as our loving Mother and fellow Christian. The *Hail Mary* remains one of our most revered and popular prayers. We know that Jesus is our Savior and principal mediator with the Father (1 Tm 2:5,6). However, because of her unique dignity and special place in salvation, Mary is a most powerful intercessor with God for the needs of his people.

11 What is the communion of saints?

The communion of saints is the union of all Christ's disciples, those who are living as well as those who are already in the next life. In this regard, a *saint* refers to anyone who is in union with Christ, not just those Christians who have been canonized saints.

In addition to its reference to the fellowship of believers, the communion of saints is a belief in the power of intercessory prayer. Those of us on earth pray and sacrifice for our dead brothers and sisters in Christ who are in the process of "purgation" to gain entrance into heaven. Meanwhile, we ask the Blessed Mother, the saints and those gone before us to pray to God for our intentions.

12 What is the role of canonized saints in our daily lives?

The church occasionally holds canonization services, at which certain persons are declared to be in heaven and formally listed among the saints. The saints remind us of our heavenly goal and inspire us to reaffirm our dedication to our own faith journey and final destiny in God.

In a number of ways various saints model for us good Christian values. These saintly heroes and heroines inspire us to practice Christian virtues. All of these holy people inspire love of God, neighbor and self. In addition, they pray for us to the Lord for our needs.

13 What are some of the ways the saints witness Christian values?

The martyrs of the church witnessed Christ in their extraordinary courage in the face of pain and suffering. They expressed an unquestioned willingness to die for Christ and our faith convictions.

We find noteworthy examples in the lives of Francis of Assisi, who shows us the importance of poverty of spirit, and Therese of Lisieux, who exemplifies the finest qualities of daily living.

Believers like Vincent de Paul and Louise de Marillac instruct us in the merits of serving the needs of the poor. The work of Elizabeth Seton and John Baptist de la Salle stressed the need for Christian-centered education. Other fine examples can be found in the work of Joan of Arc, and also Catherine of Siena, who worked to alleviate many of the world's social ills.

14 Can only canonized saints fill these *hero* and *heroine* roles?

No. There are many other people besides those who have been canonized who serve as inspirations for our lives. In our own time, women like Dorothy Day and Mother Teresa, and men like Pope John XXIII and Tom Dooley, fulfill this role very well.

15 What, then, is the communion of saints achieving?

By the saving power of Jesus Christ, the communion of saints witnesses the message of salvation, strives to be a community of love and mutual concern and reaches out to the needs of all people.

> *The communion of saints is a belief in the power of intercessory prayer.*

These goals are achieved according to the varying capacities of those in the communion.

A universal hymn of praise is given to the origin and destiny of the communion of saints by the strength of the Spirit. To this aim they sing praise to God. "Hallelujah! Salvation and glory and power to our God ..." (Rev 19:1).

A FAITH JOURNEY THROUGH THE LITURGICAL YEAR

Most Catholics are somewhat aware of the liturgical cycle known as the church year. Often that awareness is tied only to the commercial *payoff* of religious festivals and celebrations. The gift giving at Christmas, parades on St. Patrick's Day, early release from school and work on Good Friday and the commercial festivities associated with Easter are merely secular expressions of the truly dynamic nature of the church year events.

The sequence of those events is designed to help Catholics relive the events of salvation in small doses. The three-year cycle of readings provides Catholics with exposure to the major portions of sacred Scripture. In the calendar the two major liturgical seasons of Advent/Christmas and Lent/Easter/Pentecost present us with the saving words and deeds of Jesus. During these seasons we are invited to fast and reflect upon the spiritual meaning of these events, so we can undergo a spiritual and moral conversion from sinfulness to a deeper life of grace and virtue.

In addition, memorials of the saints highlight the lives of outstanding people who have witnessed to the love of Jesus in a very powerful way.

How can Catholics embrace the cycle of feasts of Christ and memorials of saints as a means to increase the dynamism of their own faith journey and spiritual growth?

A Faith Journey Through the Liturgical Year

■ A. What does the liturgical year accomplish?

In the liturgical year the various aspects of the one Paschal mystery unfold. This is also the case with the cycle of feasts surrounding the mystery of the incarnation (Annunciation, Christmas, Epiphany). They commemorate the beginning of our salvation and communicate to us the first fruits of the Paschal mystery (*Catechism*, 1171).

■ B. What is the central event of the liturgical year?

Beginning with the Easter Triduum as its source of light, the new age of the Resurrection fills the whole liturgical year with its brilliance. Gradually, on either side of this source, the year is transfigured by the liturgy. It really is a "year of the Lord's favor" (*Lk* 4:19). The economy of salvation is at work within the framework of time, but since its fulfillment in the Passover of Jesus and the outpouring of the Holy Spirit, the culmination of history is anticipated "as a foretaste," and the kingdom of God enters into our time (*Catechism*, 1168).

■ C. Why are the feast days of Mary and the saints important?

By keeping the memorials of the saints—first of all the holy Mother of God, then the apostles, the martyrs and other saints—on fixed days of the liturgical year, the Church on earth shows that she is united with the liturgy of heaven. She gives glory to Christ for having accomplished his salvation in his glorified members; their example encourages her on her way to the Father (*Catechism*, 1195).

1 What is the liturgical year?

The liturgical year is the church's annual reliving of the events of the life, death and resurrection of Jesus Christ. It is divided into the two major seasons of Advent/Christmas and Lent/Easter/Pentecost, with Ordinary Time occurring between them. Each season has a time of preparation and a time of celebration.

2 What is the meaning behind the liturgical year?

The feasts of Jesus are arranged in historical sequence, giving us an opportunity to relive the major events of his life in a prayerful and medita-

> *The feasts of Jesus are arranged in historical sequence, giving us an opportunity to relive the major events of his life in a prayerful and meditative manner.*

tive manner. Jesus is *Savior* from the moment of his incarnation. Therefore, we celebrate and experience his saving power in each of the events of the church year put before us.

By including the events within a liturgical celebration, the church helps make Christ's saving power *sacramentally* available to us. What Jesus once did in his historical ministry, he now (as risen Lord, through the Spirit) does in the mysteries of the liturgy.

3 What are the highlights of the Christmas season?

The preparation time for Christmas is *Advent,* which extends through the four Sundays before Christmas Day. During Advent we remember the people and events through which God prepared the world for the Messiah's coming. The spirit of Advent is one of anticipating Jesus, and our prayer is *Maranatha*, "Come, Lord Jesus." It is also a time for personal moral and spiritual conversion.

Our Christmas celebration begins on December 25th, when we commemorate the birth of Jesus. It continues through four other feasts, namely the Feast of the Holy Family on the Sunday after Christmas; the Feast of Mary the Mother of God on January 1; the Epiphany on January 6 (or the Sunday after Jan. 1); and the Feast of Jesus' Baptism at the Jordan River, celebrated the following Sunday.

4 Is December 25th really Jesus' birthday?

No one knows the exact day Jesus was born. Early Christians, however, wanted to celebrate the event, so they chose a day to remember and praise God for Jesus' birth.

December 25th was chosen because it is very close to the winter solstice, the shortest day of the year. In the early days of the church there was a feast celebrated by pagans to honor the "rebirth of the sun" as it begins to return after its journey away from the earth. So, too, Christians began to celebrate the birth of Jesus, "the son" who gives life, light and warmth to our lives.

5 What are the highlights of the Easter season?

The Easter season begins with the preparation period of *Lent*, which is approximately forty days long. It begins on Ash Wednesday, followed by the first Sunday of Lent, which occurs six weeks before Easter. The last week of Lent, known as *Holy Week,* begins with Passion Sunday.

6 What is the *central event* of the church year?

The central event of the church year is the *Sacred Triduum*. That is the culmination of Lent and the beginning of the Easter celebration. These three days—Holy Thursday, Good Friday and the Easter Vigil—lead us through the events of our salvation, beginning with evening Mass on Holy Thursday, through the Last Supper, the prayer and betrayal in the garden and the arrest and eventual death of Jesus.

During this time, we face the *reality* of Christ's saving death, which leads us to our celebration of Jesus' resurrection at the Easter Vigil. Holy Thursday, Good Friday and the Easter Vigil are *"one day, liturgically speaking,"* because they constitute the one saving act of Jesus' dying and rising.

The Lenten-Easter season should be thought of as one continuous celebration of the one Paschal mystery—the dying and rising of Christ and our sharing in his death and resurrection. Our celebration continues and culminates on Pentecost, the fiftieth day after Easter. We also celebrate the feast of our Lord's Ascension, ten days before Pentecost.

7 How does the church determine when Easter will be celebrated?

Easter is determined the same way as the Jewish Passover. We believe that Jesus and the apostles were celebrating Passover the night of the Last Supper, so we can compute from that date the days of his death and resurrection. The Jewish calendar is based on a lunar cycle of thirteen months, not twelve.

Therefore, Easter is determined by the moon's cycle, falling on the Sunday after the first full moon of the spring equinox.

8 What is the significance of ordinary time?

Ordinary time is the time between the seasons of Christmas and Easter. Here, we are challenged to live out the events we have prepared for and to celebrate the Eucharist with other community members.

9 What are the church's practices for liturgical seasons?

During Advent and Lent we are challenged to spend time in deep prayer and reflection on spiritual and moral matters and to fast and abstain.

> *It is possible to bring the spirit of the seasons into our family activities.*

The purpose of this is moral and spiritual conversion. Christmas and Easter raise our hearts in jubilant praise for the saving events of the Incarnation and Resurrection.

The changing focus of the liturgical year can also be seen in the decor and vestments used in churches. Colors change from somber tones of violet to joyful colors such as gold or white, and then rest with *ordinary* colors like green. Each reflects the liturgical season. Even the flowers, banners and candles displayed in church signal to the community either a penitential or joyous mood.

10 How does the Rite of Christian Initiation of Adults celebrate the church's liturgical year?

The Rite of Christian Initiation of Adults leads catechumens—and the entire church community—through a conversion process that is celebrated in the seasons of the church year. Adult initiation becomes a major experience of resurrection and new life for the church each year at the Easter Vigil.

11 How can we celebrate the liturgical seasons in our homes?

It is possible to bring the spirit of the seasons into our family activities. During Advent, families make Advent wreaths or Jesse Trees, and prepare a Christmas crib. In addition, studying the religious significance of Christmas trees, lights, candles and gift giving helps bring the true meaning of Christmas to life for many families.

To make Lent feel different from ordinary time, families can find ways to "fast" together. For example, they can give up a favorite TV program or snack or going to movies or drinking alcohol during the entire season. Projects to help the poor as a family are also an appropriate form of almsgiving. The significance of Easter eggs, new clothes and an appreciation of spring as a sign of new life should be pointed out.

During both seasons it is good practice to discuss the daily readings and to use the official church prayers for the day.

12 Are there other cycles in the church year?

There are several other ongoing cycles. They are the cycle of the saints, the daily cycle in the Prayer of Christians, lectionary cycles, weekly cycles and the cycle for holy years.

13 What is the cycle of the saints?

Each year we celebrate feast days and holy days in honor of Mary and the saints which recall the examples of these holy people. Most of these are minor feasts and pass with little notice. Among those of significance are December 8 (Immaculate Conception), August 15 (Assumption of Mary) and November 1 (All Saints Day). These days are holy days of obligation, along with Christmas, the Solemnity of Mary and Ascension Thursday.

Other important feasts include the feasts of St. Joseph (March 19, May 1), the Annunciation (March 25) and the feast of Sts. Peter and Paul (June 29). Days honoring saints of local significance such as parish, country or professional patrons also are celebrated.

14 What is the Liturgy of the Hours?

In addition to sacramental celebrations, the church engages in the custom of official communal prayer, of praising God in psalms, hymns, spiritual canticles and in morning, noon and night readings from Scripture, the church Fathers and the saints.

This is the Liturgy of the Hours, which symbolically extends the central celebration of Eucharist throughout the day. The Liturgy of the Hours flows from the altar and back to the altar, providing the church with a way of fulfilling the command of Scripture to "pray without ceasing" (1 Thess 5:17). Thus, the major segments of each day are made holy by the praise of God. This is the daily prayer of the Body of Christ, a sacrifice of praise offered around the world.

Communal prayer is an essential feature of most monasteries and convents. The Morning Praise and Evening Song (to which are added communal praise at other times) are considered to be the joyful responsibility of the church.

15 Do lay people say the Prayer of Christians?

The Prayer of Christians is the Morning Praise and Evening Song sections of the Liturgy of the Hours. Yes, many lay people participate in this prayer of the church. Often people who live near monasteries and convents are invited to join those communities in prayer. Many parishes invite interested members to gather for this prayer. Lay people also pray the Prayer of Christians in private, joining themselves in spirit with the Body of Christ around the world.

16 What are the lectionary cycles?

There are two lectionary cycles, one for Sundays and major feasts and the other for the daily cycle. Both cycles give the Scripture readings used in Catholic liturgies for specific days. With the three-year Sunday cycle (named A, B or C), and the two-year daily cycle (years 1 and 2), Catholics hear major portions of Scripture as part of their regular worship.

Further study and reflection on Sunday readings provides an excellent way to increase our awareness of Scripture.

17 What is the importance of Sunday?

Sunday is supposed to be like a "little Easter" as we gather to celebrate the Lord's resurrection.

> *Sunday is supposed to be like a little Easter.*

Even in penitential seasons, Sunday is never a *fast* day but a *feast* day.

18 How does the natural cycle affect the church year?

Nature's cycle affects the language of prayers. Winter, snow, short days and the winter solstice provide strong images for the Advent-Christmas cycle. Spring flowers and talk of sunshine permeate the Easter language. Harvest images appear in the last judgment themes near the end of the church year.

Unfortunately, Catholics living in the Southern Hemisphere cannot identify with this because of the reversal of seasons. For them, there is no correspondence with their natural cycle and the church year.

DEATH SHALL HAVE NO DOMINION

Death is an unavoidable fact of life for each of us, regardless of our age or position in life. Newspapers and broadcasts present us with daily accounts of death, which often occurs violently in massacres, murders, suicides, abortions, assassinations, holocausts, infanticides and acts of terrorism and war.

While on trial for treason, Thomas More said, "Death comes for us all, my lords. Yes, even for kings. Amid their royalty and brute strength, death will neither kneel nor make any reverence. Death will roughly grasp them by the very breast and rattle them till they be stark dead."

Throughout history poets, philosophers and religious teachers have attempted to make some sense of the eventuality of death. Poet John Donne wrote that death teaches us about our common humanity. "Do not send to know for whom the bell tolls. It tolls for thee. No man is an island unto himself."

It is the church, however, that comes to grips with the abiding mystery of death. The belief in the resurrection of Jesus serves as a cornerstone of the church's conviction that death shall have no dominion. It is that religious belief and hope that provides the spirit for this topic.

Death Shall Have No Dominion

■ A. Why did death come about?
In a sense bodily death is natural, but for faith it is in fact "the wages of sin" (*Rom* 6:23) ... *Death is a consequence of sin.* The Church's Magisterium, as authentic interpreter of the affirmations of Scripture and Tradition, teaches that death entered the world on account of man's sin. Even though man's nature is mortal, God had destined him not to die. Death was therefore contrary to the plans of God the Creator and entered the world as a consequence of sin (*Catechism*, 1006, 1008).

■ B. What is the meaning of Christian death?
Because of Christ, Christian death has a positive meaning: "For to me to live is Christ, and to die is gain" (*Phil* 1:21). "The saying is sure: if we have died with him, we will also live with him" (*2 Tm* 2:11). What is essentially new about Christian death is this: through Baptism, the Christian has already "died with Christ" sacramentally, in order to live a new life; and if we die in Christ's grace, physical death completes this "dying with Christ" and so completes our incorporation into him in his redeeming act (*Catechism*, 1010).

■ C. How should we prepare for death?
"Every action of yours, every thought, should be those of one who expects to die before the day is out. Death would have no great terrors for you if you had a quiet conscience. . . Then why not keep clear of sin instead of running away from death? If you aren't fit to face death today, it's very unlikely you will be tomorrow" (Thomas a' Kempis, *The Imitation of Christ*, 1,23,1) (*Catechism*, 1014).

1 What does death teach us?

Death is the cancellation of all our possibilities and activities on earth. It urges us to form coherent, purposeful lives while we are alive. In addition, in anticipation of our own death, we should carefully evaluate our lives and organize our resources and energies in a useful manner.

2 What does the Bible give as the reason for death?

Death is the consequence of sin. "... sin came into the world through one man, and death came

> *It is the church that comes to grips with the abiding mystery of death.*

through sin, and so death spread to all because all have sinned ..." (Rom 5:12).

We are also told that "As all die in Adam, so all will be made alive in Christ" (1 Cor 15:22).

3 How do we as human beings face death?

The studies of Dr. Elizabeth Kubler-Ross offer a picture of how we deal with death. She speaks of five stages of dying. They are:

■ a) *Denial*: Subconsciously, we tend to believe we are immortal, and that we will not die. This attitude is reinforced by our society.

■ b) *Anger*: We are likely to become angry when faced with the eventuality of our own death. In the words of the poet Dylan Thomas, "Rage, rage, against the dying of the light."

■ c) *Bargaining*: When the anger dies down, often we become cunning and try to bargain with God for more time on earth. Often humans promise virtuous behavior, saying, "O God, I will never say another unkind word, if you will but spare me."

■ d) *Depression:* Eventually, we become tired of the battle, and depression sets in. One may die with dignity, but may not avoid its indignities, such as the loss of control over our bodily functions.

■ e) *Acceptance:* Finally, peace sets in and we accept our death. Before his death, Pope John XXIII said, "My bags are packed. I am ready to go." In order to be *ready,* we must loosen the ties that bound us to this life.

4 How does the Bible suggest Christians face death?

Scripture teaches that we should not deny the existence of death. We are told to have faith and hope in our own individual resurrections, because Jesus conquered death for us and showed us there is an eternal life awaiting us.

Scripture writers have addressed the question of death. From them we learn that Christ "abolished death and brought life and immortality to light through the gospel" (2 Tm 1:10). And: "if we have died with Christ, we believe that we will also live with him" (Rom 6:8).

As we read the consoling story of the resurrection of Lazarus, we learn that Christ is the "... resurrection and the life. Those who believe in me, even though they die, will live ..." (Jn 11:25).

5 What is the teaching of the Second Vatican Council on death?

The *Pastoral Constitution on the Church in the Modern World* states, "It is in the face of death that the riddle of human existence becomes most acute ... All the endeavors of technology, though useful in the extreme, cannot calm his anxiety" (No. 18).

Only faith and hope can overcome our anxieties about death. God summons us to an endless sharing of divine life beyond all corruption. Jesus has won this for us by his death and resurrection.

6 Can death have inspirational value?

For some secular philosophers death is treated as a meaningless, absurd subject. In fact, the deaths of some individuals, especially the Christian martyrs, have proved to be courageous events of enduring inspiration. This is clearly the case in the death of Father Maximilian Kolbe, who volunteered to die in the place of a family man while both were prisoners at the Auschwitz concentration camp during World War II. The priest's death was an inspiring affront to the degrading, dehumanizing intent of the camps. He is now a canonized saint of the church.

The greatest death in history, that of Jesus Christ, both inspires us and redeems us from the fears and anxieties we have about death.

7 What does the New Testament teach us about our final judgment?

The New Testament teaches that judgment is an act of God, determining whether we have lived faithful, honest, sincere and moral lives in our earthly pilgrimage. There are numerous texts which describe the various dimensions of the judgment day.

One such text tells us that "... if you are angry with a brother or sister, you will be liable to judgment; ... and if you say, 'You fool' you will be liable to the hell of fire" (Mt 5:22). From Romans we learn that "... God, through Jesus Christ, will judge the secret thoughts of all" (2:16).

And from John, we are told firmly that "Those who believe in him are not condemned; but those who do not believe are condemned already, because they have not believed in the name of the only Son of God" (Jn 3:18).

8 How do the Apostles' and Nicene creeds speak of judgment?

The Apostles' Creed addresses judgment in the statement, "He shall come again to judge the living and the dead." The Nicene Creed declares, "He ascended into heaven and shall come again to judge the living and the dead."

9 What is the difference between "general" and "particular" judgment?

The Catholic Church teaches that there will be a second coming of Jesus Christ at the end of time,

> *The trumpet will sound, and the dead will be raised imperishable.*

and that he will judge the living and the dead. This is the general judgment which affects all people, and the *last* judgment, because it terminates the history of the world.

At the same time we, as unique individuals, will have particular judgments. Preparation for this action gives meaning and purpose during our lives and for our deaths. At our particular judgments Jesus will evaluate each of us individually according to our faith, hope, love and moral witness, and treat us accordingly.

10 What is purgatory?

From its beginning the Catholic Church has taught that there is a state of *purgation* after death. Since the dead cannot help themselves to attain everlasting peace, they can benefit from the prayers of the living. Today, we pray for the dead at liturgy, directing our prayers toward their purgation. Our attention is especially drawn toward this intention on November 2 when we celebrate the Feast of All Souls.

We believe that while in *purgatory* the person enters a process which cleanses him or her from selfishness and thus helps the person acquire the love necessary to be in full unity with God. While it is believed to be a painful process, it is one that promises enormous growth. Much joy is promised in this state, because the person is being made ready for union with the Father.

Prayers for the dead constitute a sharing of love by those on earth for those who have died. These prayers assist them to attain heaven more quickly. Not all who die will go through purgation. Some people leave this life with the kind of love of God, neighbor and self that admits them immediately into eternal glory.

11 What are indulgences?

Pope Paul VI said indulgences are "the remission, in the sight of God, of the temporal punishment due to sins which have already been blotted out as far as guilt is concerned."

Indulgences may either be plenary (full remission) or partial. The individual gaining the indulgence should be sincere in seeking forgiveness. Pope Paul VI tied this teaching to the communion of saints and the abiding sense of responsibility the living have for their dead relatives and friends. We should not liken the treasury of the church to a "hoard of material wealth," but to the infinite and inexhaustible value which the expiation and merits of Christ have in the sight of God.

12 What is the resurrection of the body?

Biblical texts indicate that our bodily resurrection will occur at the last judgment and the coming of Christ. At that time, the whole person is to be saved. That means our body as well as our soul and spirit.

St. Paul tells us that "The trumpet will sound, and the dead will be raised imperishable" (1 Cor 15:52). In the Apostles' and Nicene creeds we state that we "believe in the resurrection of the body." The church teaches that this event already occurred for Jesus at Easter and for Mary at her assumption into heaven (cf. all of 1 Cor 15).

13 What is hell?

Hell is the name given to the state reserved for those who die completely turned away from God. They will remain in pain and unhappiness forever. Jesus spoke of hell when he said, "You that are accursed, depart from me into the eternal fire prepared for the devil and his angels" (Mt 25:41; cf. Mt 13:36 - 43; 2 Thes 1:7-10).

The word "hell" is derived from the German *hel,* which means the realm of the dead. Both Jesus and the church teach the existence of hell. If someone *deliberately* rejects God, he or she chooses hell—a totally isolated existence in which one is estranged from God.

14 What is heaven?

We believe heaven is an eternal life or beatific vision of unending union with God. We expect that in heaven we will be in the company of the angels and saints, the saved.

Scripture describes heaven. "The home of God is among mortals. He will dwell with them as their

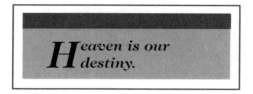

Heaven is our destiny.

God; they will be his peoples, and God himself will be with them; ... death will be no more; mourning and crying and pain will be no more, for the first things have passed away" (Rv 21:3,4).

Heaven is our destiny. It is the final stage of our faith journey, the ultimate goal of our existence. God offers us the power and love to achieve this destiny through the grace of Jesus. St. Paul tells us that we shall see God "face to face" (1 Cor 13:12), and that "No eye has seen, nor ear heard, nor the human heart conceived, what God has prepared for those who love him" (1 Cor 2:9).

15 How is the Christian view of death illustrated in the Mass of Christian Burial?

During the Mass of Christian Burial, two symbols capture our attention. They are the presence of the Easter candle and the white cloth which covers the casket. They are reminders of the sacrament of baptism, at which time the person began his or her faith journey.

The funeral celebration commemorates the last moments of the person's earthly pilgrimage and the first moments of his or her entry into eternal life. During the Mass much attention is paid to the elements of faith and hope in the future life, thereby consoling the mourning relatives and friends.

I BELIEVE ... WE BELIEVE IN GOD

"Faith is a personal act—the free response of the human person to the initiative of God who reveals himself. But faith is not an isolated act. No one can believe alone, just as no one can live alone. You have not given yourself faith as you have not given yourself life. The believer has received faith from others and should hand it on to others. Our love for Jesus and for our neighbor impels us to speak to others about our faith. Each believer is thus a link in the great chain of believers. I cannot believe without being carried by the faith of others, and by my faith I help support others in the faith" (*Catechism*, 166).

The *Catechism* notes both the personal and communal aspects of faith, the "I believe" and the "We believe." The Apostles' Creed begins with "I believe" and the Nicene Creed begins with "We believe." Thus faith is a personal matter, because each Catholic must make an act of faith and embark on a lifelong journey of faith. At the same time, no Catholic walks alone, for every Catholic is united with the community of believers. Each of us is a person in communion with the People of God and the Body of Christ.

All faith is a response to the revelation of God, who both revealed himself as a Trinity of Father, Son and Spirit and proclaimed the message of salvation in his divine plan of love for us. Hence our Christian life is a dialogue which begins with God's revelation and includes our faith response to that revelation. Our faith is always a gift from the Holy Spirit, who gives us faith, helps us to develop it and brings us to perfection in it.

I Believe ... We Believe in God

■ A. What is the obedience of faith?

To obey (from the Latin ob-audire, to "hear or listen to") in faith is to submit freely to the word that has been heard, because its truth is guaranteed by God, who is Truth itself. Abraham is the model of such obedience

offered us by Sacred Scripture. The Virgin Mary is its most perfect embodiment. The *Letter to the Hebrews*, in its great eulogy of the faith of Israel's ancestors, lays special emphasis on Abraham's faith: "By faith, Abraham obeyed when he was called to go out to a place which he was to receive as an inheritance; and he went out, not knowing where he was to go" (*Heb* 11:8) (*Catechism*, 144-145).

■ B. Is faith a divine gift?

When St. Peter confessed that Jesus is the Christ, the Son of the living God, Jesus declared to him that this revelation did not come "from flesh and blood," but from "my Father who is in heaven" (*Mt* 16:17). *Faith is a gift of God, a supernatural virtue infused by him* (*Catechism*, 153).

■ C. Is faith a human act?

Believing is possible only by grace and the interior helps of the Holy Spirit. But it is no less true that believing is an authentically human act. Trusting in God and cleaving to the truths he has revealed is contrary neither to human freedom nor to human reason ... In faith, the human intellect and will cooperate with divine grace: "Believing is an act of the intellect assenting to the divine truth by command of the will moved by God through grace" (St. Thomas Aquinas, *Summa II-II, 2,9*) (*Catechism*, 154-155).

1 How does St. Paul describe faith?

Paul described faith as the "... assurance of things hoped for, the conviction of things not seen" (Heb 11:1). He also tells us that "For one believes with the heart and so is justified, and one confesses with the mouth and so is saved" (Rom 10:10) and that the Lord's justice "has been disclosed" (Rom 3:21).

2 What conclusions can we draw about faith from these texts?

We can derive three insights from St. Paul's teachings. First, that faith is an act of *trust* and *hope*, a positive spiritual attitude toward life and God. Second, that faith leads us to accept salvation, love and forgiveness from God. And third, that faith is a commitment to Christ, through whom salvation from God has been manifested and accomplished.

3 Does St. Paul teach religious truths?

In his First Letter to Timothy, Paul writes, "If you put these instructions before the brothers and sisters, you will be a good servant of Christ Jesus, nourished on the words of the faith and of the sound teaching that you have followed" (4:6).

4 Where may we find examples of faith in the Gospel?

In the Gospel of Mark, we find that from the very beginning of his ministry, Jesus preached, "The kingdom of God has come near; repent, and believe in the good news" (1:15). In the story of

> *In faith, the human intellect and will cooperate with divine grace.*

the cure of the possessed boy, faith is described as the quality of having sufficient trust in Jesus' power to perform miracles. In this story, the boy's father exclaimed, "I believe; help my unbelief!" (Mk 9:24).

John's Gospel often emphasized our need to surrender in faith to Jesus. "Believe in God, believe also in me" (14:1). In the Bread of Life Discourse, Jesus said, "The words that I have spoken to you are spirit and life" (Jn 6:63). Hearing Christ's words, Peter, speaking for the others, committed himself to the Lord, saying, "... to whom can we go? You have the words of eternal life. We have come to believe and know that you are the Holy One of God" (Jn 6:68).

5 How does the New Testament link faith to Christian behavior?

Jesus used the image of the vine and branches to tie faith to deeds. He said, "I am the vine, you are the branches. Those who abide in me and I in them bear much fruit" (Jn 15:5). Practical-minded St. James drew a vivid connection for us when he said "For just as the body without the spirit is dead, so faith without works is also dead" (Jas 2:26).

The parable of the sower provides another good example for us to follow. "But as for that in the good soil, these are the ones who, when they hear the word, hold it fast in an honest and good heart, and bear fruit with patient endurance" (Lk 8:15).

6 How does faith originate?

God has created us to be people of faith. He has put the potential for faith deep within each of us. We find ourselves driven to know and love without limits and to be known and loved. With this drive we search for the very infinite God. God gives us the gift of faith to make this possible.

St. Augustine speaks of this as our restless heart, which is not satisfied with anyone less than God. The Father is equally reaching out to us to fulfill the spiritual hunger and thirst he has given us. "I have loved you with an everlasting love ..." (Jer 31:3). Just as a lover tries to evoke a response in his or her beloved, so does God seek to awaken us to respond to him.

7 What is revelation?

Revelation is the act of God which discloses his affectionate presence to us for the purpose of awakening our faith response. *Grace* is the name given to describe God's work of giving us the potential for faith and then prompting its actualization.

8 How does God reveal himself to us in Scripture?

God speaks to us through the Old Testament judges, kings, priests, prophets, sages and biblical writers. We hear his voice as he speaks to Moses, Miriam, Joshua, Deborah, David and many others. God inspired the biblical authors to record the words and deeds of his revelation.

The Father reaches out to us, above all, in his Son, Jesus Christ. "He is the image of the invisible

God ..." (Col 1:15). From the Word made flesh we hear the words of God, the message of salvation and the call to faith. In Christ we experience revelation in its richest form and are summoned to respond in faith.

Scripture tells us that God will reserve the final revelation of himself to us for the end of time when "... the Son of Man will appear in heaven ... with power and great glory," to judge the living and the dead (Mt 24:30).

9 What form does our faith take in relation to nature?

God speaks to us through his providential presence in nature. "The heavens are telling the glory of God ... Day to day pours forth speech, and night to night declares knowledge (of God) ..." (Ps 19:1-2). Nature is a window unto the sacred. It is filled with

> *Faith is a commitment to Christ.*

the mystery of God. Before industrialization, people lived on farms, dwelling in harmony with nature. People were in touch with the "secret ministry of the frost," as the author Coleridge tells us. With the development of cities people now live in a man-made environment. We are often out of touch with nature, and our *sense of wonder* is asleep.

When we are alive, however, to nature's hymn to the Creator, our faith takes the shape of wonder again. We are at home then with the words of the psalmist who asked nature to "Praise him, sun and moon ... all you shining stars ... Praise him ... mountains and all hills, fruit trees and all cedars! Wild animals and all cattle, creeping things and flying birds" (148:3,4,9,10).

Thus, faith-wonder helps us to sense the *holiness* of creation. We reverence the environment and do not exploit it.

10 How should we receive the mystery of God through our faith experience?

When we are faced with the mystery of God, faith takes the form of awe. Biblical translations sometimes use the word *fear*, which has come to mean the paralyzing emotion that causes us to run away

from God in terror. Awe, however, deals with sensitivity to the presence of the mystery of God and a reverence that results from an honest appreciation of oneself before the magnificent purity of God (cf. Is 6).

The writer of Hebrews reminds us that "Therefore, since we are receiving a kingdom that cannot be shaken, let us give thanks, by which we offer to God an acceptable worship with reverence and awe" (12:28).

11 What is there about the mystery of God that causes faith to become awe?

We can consider mystery under three aspects:
■ a) God's mystery is both *known* and *unknown*. Thomas Aquinas spoke of the darkness of God. He said that "since our mind is not proportionate to the divine substance, that which is the substance of God remains beyond our intellects and unknown to us. Hence, the supreme knowledge which man has of God is to know that he does not know God, in so far as he knows *what* God *is* surpasses all that we can understand of him."

Nevertheless, God is also *light*. He chooses to give us knowledge of *who* he is in the Old and New Testaments, the church and above all in Jesus Christ. This revelation helps us perceive his presence in acts of love and in the signs of the times. In this process, the mystery of God is an *unknown* that gradually comes to be *known*.
■ b) Mystery is a *universal* experience. We would be better able to appreciate the mystery of God if we were more attuned to the mystery of life and the universe itself. Even the storehouse of scientific knowledge obtained to date is not sufficient to grasp the facts of our surroundings. Only with faith and reverence for the environment can we perceive the mystery of life.
■ c) Mystery *reveals* and *conceals*. God does not remain in repose. Rather, he wishes to enter the lives of his people. The mystery moves toward disclosure. This is the rhythm of revealing and concealing. It keeps alive our pursuit of that which is yet to be known and experienced about God.

As we proceed through life we are given glimpses of glory and times of darkness. Faith and conviction move us onward to deeper appreciation of God's love. We cannot drink in the whole meaning of God all at once. It takes reflection and is a lifelong growth experience.

12 What role does faith awe play in our lives?

Faith awe is our spontaneous response to the mystery of God. It engenders in us the thirst for wisdom which is less interested in the practical necessities of life and more concerned with the meaning and purpose of life.

Today, people with scientific views of life think that the meaning of life can only be acquired by one's own efforts. We tend to *make* meanings, whereas a person who has a sense of faith awe *receives* meanings as a grace from God.

There is no contradiction here, for God intends us to do both. He gave us intelligence to make sense out of our world and faith awe to discover meaning about the world that only he can reveal. When the two approaches are in harmony, wisdom is the result.

13 What does the Bible tell us about the glory of God?

Mystery emphasizes that aspect of God that is yet to be known and experienced. The glory of God comes through as light, warmth, guidance, love, affection, surprise and self-discovery. His glory lights up our world and gives us guidance and meaning.

When Isaiah beheld the glory of God in the Temple (Is 6), he experienced self-discovery and conversion. Moses received the same gift at the burning bush and Ezekiel rejoiced in this event at the Chebar River visions. God's glory was most completely manifested when Jesus walked on the earth. How strong Jesus' impact on the apostles,

Mary Magdalen and the centurion at the cross must have been! Christ's glory became most evident in his Easter appearances to the apostles and disciples. The divine glory speaks of the extraordinary intimacy by which God enters our inner life.

14 What implications does the glory of God have for our faith?

The theme of the divine glory reminds us that God is just as anxious to get in touch with us as we are to be in touch with him. The glory of God is his active presence which strives to make itself felt in human beings.

> *Nature is a window unto the sacred.*

Faith commitment is our response to the glory presence of God. John's Gospel emphasizes the theme of glory as identified with Jesus. All that Jesus does is a sign of the presence of God reaching out to his people. That is why Jesus asks Peter over and over again, "Do you love me?" Jesus aches for that kind of faith commitment from Peter. And, praise the Lord, Peter gives that faith commitment that is to be our model.

PRAISE THE LORD

All prayer begins with God. "God calls man first. Man may forget his Creator or hide far from his face; he may run after idols or accuse the deity of having abandoned him; yet the living and true God tirelessly calls each person to that mysterious encounter known as prayer. In prayer, the faithful God's initiative of love always comes first; our own first step is always a response. As God gradually reveals himself and reveals man to himself, prayer appears as a reciprocal call, a covenant drama. Through words and actions, this drama engages the heart. It unfolds throughout the whole history of salvation" (*Catechism*, 2567).

One of the greatest examples of prayer that we have is the Book of Psalms, God's revelation of what prayer should be like. In the Psalms, prayer is always sustained by praise. That is why the book is referred to as "The Praises."

"What is more pleasing than a psalm? David expresses it well: 'Praise the Lord, for a song of praise is good: Let there be praise of God with gladness and grace!' Yes, a psalm is a blessing on the lips of the people, a hymn in praise of God, the assembly's homage, a general acclamation, a word that speaks for all, the voice of the Church, a confession of faith in song" (St. Ambrose, *Explanation of Psalms*, 1, 9).

Praise the Lord

■ A. How did Jesus learn to pray?
The Son of God who became Son of the Virgin learned to pray in his human heart. He learns to pray from his mother, who kept all the great things the Almighty had done and treasured them in her heart. He learns to pray in the words and rhythms of the prayer of his people, in the synagogue at Nazareth and the Temple at Jerusalem. But his prayer springs from an otherwise secret source, as he intimates at the age of twelve: "I must be in my Father's house" (*Lk* 2:49). Here the newness of prayer in

the fullness of time begins to be revealed: his *filial prayer*, which the Father awaits from his children, is finally going to be lived out by the only Son in his humanity, with and for men (*Catechism*, 2599).

■ B. How did Jesus teach us to pray?
When Jesus prays he is already teaching us how to pray. His prayer to his Father is the theologal path (the path of faith, hope and charity) of our prayer to God. But the Gospel also gives us Jesus' explicit teaching on prayer. Like a wise teacher he takes hold of us where we are and leads us progressively toward the Father. Addressing the crowds following him, Jesus builds on what they already know of prayer from the Old Covenant and opens to them the newness of the coming Kingdom. Then he reveals this newness to them in parables. Finally, he will speak openly of the Father and the Holy Spirit to his disciples who will be the teachers of prayer in his Church (*Catechism*, 2607).

■ C. What shall we say of the "Our Father"?
In response to his disciples' request "Lord, teach us to pray" (*Lk* 11:1), Jesus entrusts them with the fundamental Christian prayer, the Our Father. "The Lord's Prayer is truly the summary of the whole gospel" (Tertullian), the "most perfect of prayers" (St. Thomas Aquinas). It is at the center of the Scriptures ... The Lord's Prayer is the quintessential prayer of the Church (*Catechism*, 2773, 2774, 2776).

1 What is prayer?

Prayer is the experience of meeting God in conversation, words or even in silence. It is a moment of quiet wonder, which may be accompanied by hymns and gestures of affection for the Lord. Sometimes the event of prayer soars in

> **Prayer is the experience of meeting God.**

ecstasy. Most of the time, however, it is like the "old shoe comfort" of a couple quietly at home with each other. Real prayer is always directed to God.

2 Why do people pray?

Once one has surrendered himself or herself to Christ in faith and experienced the return of our Lord's love, prayer is inevitable. We pray to God because we are *in love* with him and have experienced his love in return. Prayer is then an expression of a divine-human love event. We should acquire the habit of prayer and we also have the responsibility to pray always (1 Thess 5:17).

Tragedy and sorrow frequently move us to pray, often only when the situation seems completely hopeless. Crises also have the capacity to awaken us to the power of prayer. The motives for prayer are as wide-ranging as human ingenuity itself. But love of God would motivate us to pray always.

3 What is the value of prayer words, hymns or gestures?

The words, rituals and hymns of prayer have a sacred character. They are windows onto the sacred and trails we can follow to enter the holy clearing where our faith-filled ancestors were privileged to have access.

These prayer *formulas* are the residue of a people's encounter with God. For example, the psalms are an institutional memory and expression of a people of faith and their rendezvous with God. The words of the psalms have a resonance with the divine and intimations of a loving communion with the Lord. Psalm words, like rituals and hymns, wake us up to the glorious presence of God striving to reach us.

4 Why do we need to practice meditative prayer?

Meditation concentrates on the role of the *heart* in prayer. This does not exclude the activity of the mind; rather, it moves the mind to a more restful state of contemplation of God. Through meditation we are introduced to the inwardness that allows us to put our whole heart into prayer words, hymns and gestures. Without it, we run the risk of formalism in our liturgies and common and personal prayers.

By meditating, we save public prayer from being a dry stalk. Some spiritual guides say that it may take as much as one hour of meditation to enter the prayer of the heart that unites our soul to prayer words or hymns used for public prayer.

But at the same time, formal and devotional, spoken or sung, prayers can lead us to meditation. Meditation and formal prayers complement one another.

5 Should we rely on our urge to pray, or should we engage in regular prayer time?

We need both. Regular, daily prayer may run the risk of becoming routine and cause us to lapse into formalism, while waiting for inspiration to pray may result in our never praying at all. To rely solely on regularity could dry up our spirit, and we would never meet God.

The Catholic tradition is to reiterate the ritual words and gestures shaped over the centuries of our history in order to meet the Spirit over and over again. This happens especially in the Eucharist and the Liturgy of the Hours. The very act of going to our houses of worship every day or on Sunday is a recommitment to God. Our personal life of meditation nourishes the prayer of the heart and provides us with the inward peace we need for prayer.

6 Should we concentrate on ourselves or on God when we pray?

Prayer is an event of relating between ourselves and God. As in any relationship, prayer usually begins with self-awareness and the preparations necessary to be open to the coming of the Lord into our hearts. As we move into a spirit of expectation, we become blessed with his presence. Our concentration shifts to God, because his inherent attractiveness solicits our attention, and we are lost in wonder.

7 Is prayer the same as thinking deep thoughts?

Profound thinking about divine topics is not the same as prayer. Calculated thinking can be as prized a thrill for us as that of an athlete who takes delight in muscle power and physical agility. Mental agility, however, is not the same as praying.

We must guard against the illusion that contact with disembodied thought about spiritual truths serves as prayer. Thinking great or even holy thoughts is not the same as meeting God. In fact, the outcome could be that the profound thinker would merely be creating his or her own God, instead of being shaped and renewed by the living God.

8 Is prayer the same as having religious feelings?

Feelings, whether exalting or superficial, do not automatically mean that we have an audience with God. Pleasant religious feelings may or may not accompany real prayer. The example of many of our saints advises us to seek the God of consolation, not the consolations of God.

It is popular today to speak of the need for religious experience. But the term "experience"

> **We seek to meet God with patience, persistence and spiritual discipline.**

can be misleading for those who live in a culture where constant emotional stimulation at a surface level is the norm. Feelings may range from simple "pins and needles" to "Grand Canyon speechlessness." Too many people identify simply being *stunned* as a profound experience.

A deeper reason for emotional apathy is the loss of fidelity to long-lasting love relationships. As a result, too many people stagger from one stimulation to the next, sipping from the cup of life but never drinking deeply. In the words of poet Ernest Dowson, "I cried for madder music and thirsted for stronger wine."

A religious experience is like a deepening love relationship. In each instance we are on a voyage, much the way we would be on a sailboat, silently catching the wind. We seek to meet God with patience, persistence and spiritual discipline. There will be times when the person is so directly in touch with God that feelings do not matter. We should remember that all prayer, like faith, is a gift

of the Holy Spirit who moves us to pray, presides over our prayer and brings it to fulfillment.

9 What obstacle do we face in our efforts to secure the concentration needed for prayer?

The environment in which we live holds a higher regard for distraction than for concentration. Today's communications revolution causes many people to be hooked on news and entertainment. We have forgotten how to retire from the noise and how to seek to make sense, meaning and purpose out of the noise that seems to be everywhere around us.

In the words of Teresa of Avila, our minds have become like "a drunken monkey or (like) an unbroken horse." Too many people turn to tranquilizers, sex or drink for momentary relief for their upset minds and aching souls. In fact, they are choosing the short term dulling of an ache over the long term cure of the cause.

10 Are guides available to help us learn to concentrate our inner resources?

The rich tradition of the Catholic Church possesses resources that can be helpful for spiritual discipline and the habit of inwardness. The *Exercises of St. Ignatius* provides an excellent guide for concentrating our inner resources. With these exercises we can learn to interweave our own thinking and yearning with a faith that learns how to rest in the presence of the Lord and to take note of God's inner direction.

St. Teresa takes another approach. She takes us through stages of spiritual growth or "loves." In the first love, we encounter both a joyous beginning and our first obstacles that help purify our love. In our second love, we begin our lifelong journey in identifying with Christ, a trip marked by peaks of light and valleys of darkness. In our third love, we arrive at a stable, simple union with God where we are not self-conscious about our relationship with God.

11 Are there any other such works to help us develop our prayer life?

Yes. In the tradition of St. Benedict we have the riches of liturgical prayer and meditative readings of the Bible, as well as spiritual authors. In these readings we are taught how to get in touch with the prayer of the heart. Thus, in the rhythm of liturgy, common prayer and divine reading, we are brought to inwardness that leads to stable prayer. Further information on approaches to prayer may be found at Catholic libraries and religious bookstores.

12 How can we choose the method of prayer that is best for us?

Selecting a method of prayer is like selecting clothing. We usually pick clothing that suits our temperament and meets the demands of the day.

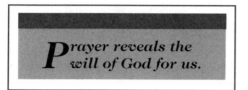

Prayer reveals the will of God for us.

We should search in faith and patience for what is best and never forget that a method is a *means* to an *end*. A prayerful meeting with God is our goal; the methods are possible routes we can take.

Whatever method we choose for prayer, we are emptying our souls of needless preoccupations so that we may be filled with God. We shut off our minds, bodies and emotions, in order to be open to the Spirit. We alter our mind states that we may have God alter our soul states. We cease to seek self-induced energy as we open ourselves to God-induced energy. The method is *not* the message, but the means to an end.

13 Why doesn't God answer all our prayers?

In the *Our Father* we pray, "Thy will be done." When Jesus told us to seek and we shall find, he was teaching us that prayer reveals the will of God for us. That will is full of love and care. God is always answering our prayers, but an answer may be a loving *no* as well as a loving *yes*.

In the story of Job, bad things happen to a good man. He prayed to have these things taken away, but the more he prayed, the more he realized what it is like to be in touch with God's loving will. "I know that my Redeemer lives ... then in my flesh I shall see God" (Jb 19:25,26). However mysterious God's will may be, it discloses that he was on Job's side.

God may not still all the storms that face us, but he will still the storms in our hearts. At Gethsemane, Jesus showed us the truest goal of prayer. He asked that the cup of suffering be taken away. Then, he concluded his prayer with a phrase from the Our Father, that of "Thy will be done."

APPENDIX

Important Prayers for Catholics

The Sign of the Cross

In the name of the Father, and of the Son, and of the Holy Spirit. Amen.

Our Father (Lord's Prayer)

Our Father, who art in heaven, hallowed be thy name; thy kingdom come; thy will be done on earth as it is in heaven. Give us this day our daily bread; and forgive us our trespasses as we forgive those who trespass against us; and lead us not into temptation, but deliver us from evil. (For thine is the kingdom and the power and the glory forever and ever.) Amen.

Hail Mary

Hail Mary, full of grace. The Lord is with you. Blessed are you among women, and blessed is the fruit of your womb, Jesus. Holy Mary, Mother of God, pray for us sinners, now and at the hour of our death. Amen.

Prayer of Praise

Glory to the Father, and to the Son, and to the Holy Spirit; as it was in the beginning, is now and will be for ever. Amen.

Prayer of the Holy Spirit

Come Holy Spirit, fill the hearts of your faithful, and enkindle in us the fire of your divine love. Send forth your spirit and we shall be created, and you shall renew the face of the earth.
O God who instructed the hearts of the faithful by the light of your divine Spirit, grant us by that same spirit to be truly wise and to rejoice in your holy consolation through the same Christ, our Lord. Amen.

Act of Contrition

My God, I am sorry for my sins with all my heart. In choosing to do wrong and failing to do good, I have sinned against you whom I should love above all things. I firmly intend, with your help, to do penance, to sin no more, and to avoid whatever leads me to sin. Our Savior Jesus Christ suffered and died for us. In his name, my God, have mercy.

(Rite of Reconciliation)

Apostles' Creed

I believe in God the Father Almighty, Creator of heaven and earth; and in Jesus Christ, his only Son, our Lord. He was conceived by the power of the Holy Spirit, and born of the Virgin Mary. He suffered under Pontius Pilate, was crucified, died, and was buried. He descended to the dead. On the third day he arose again. He ascended to heaven, and is seated at the right hand of the Father. He will come again to judge the living and the dead. I believe in the Holy Spirit, the holy Catholic Church, the Communion of Saints, the forgiveness of sins, the resurrection of the body, and life everlasting. Amen.

Act of Faith

O my God, I firmly believe that you are one God in three divine persons, Father, Son and Holy Spirit; I believe that your Divine Son became man and died for our sins, and that he will come to judge the living and the dead. I believe these and all the truths which the holy Catholic Church teaches, because you revealed them, who can neither deceive nor be deceived. Amen.

Act of Hope

O my God, trusting in your promises and the infinite merits of Jesus Christ our Redeemer, I hope for the pardon of my sins and the graces I need to serve you faithfully on earth and to obtain eternal life in heaven. Amen.

Act of Love

O my God, I love you above all things, with my whole heart and soul, because you are infinitely good and deserving of all my love. I love my neighbor as myself for love of you. Amen.

Morning Offering

O Jesus, through the Immaculate Heart of Mary, I offer you my prayers, works, joys, and sufferings of this day in union with the holy sacrifice of the Mass throughout the world. I offer them for all the intentions of your Sacred Heart. Amen.

Grace Before Meals

Bless us, O Lord, and these your gifts which we are about to receive from your bounty, through Christ our Lord. Amen.

Grace After Meals

We give you thanks, almighty God, for all your benefits, who live and reign now and forever. Amen.

The Rosary

The rosary is an important prayer in Catholic tradition. It involves vocal prayers (*Apostles' Creed, Our Father, Hail Mary, Prayer of Praise*), meditative prayer (on the mysteries of the rosary), and usually the use of rosary beads as an individual or a group of people say the rosary.

Mysteries of the Rosary

Joyful Mysteries — events surrounding the birth and early life of Jesus

Annunciation
Visitation
Birth of Jesus
Presentation in the Temple
Finding the Child Jesus in the Temple

Sorrowful Mysteries — events surrounding the passion and death of Jesus

Agony in the Garden
Scourging at the Pillar
Crowning with Thorns
Jesus Carries His Cross
Death of Jesus on the Cross

Glorious Mysteries — events and faith of the early church's experience

Resurrection of Jesus from the Tomb
Ascension into Heaven
Descent of the Holy Spirit upon the Apostles
Assumption of Mary to Heaven
Coronation of Mary as Queen of Heaven and Earth

Seven Sacraments in the Catholic Church

Baptism
Confirmation
Eucharist (Communion)
Reconciliation (Penance, Confession)
Anointing of the Sick (formerly called Extreme Unction)
Marriage
Holy Orders

Theological Virtues

Faith
Hope
Love

Cardinal Virtues

Prudence
Justice
Temperance
Fortitude

Gifts of the Holy Spirit

Wisdom
Understanding
Counsel
Fortitude
Knowledge
Piety
Fear of the Lord

Fruits of the Holy Spirit

Charity
Joy
Peace
Patience
Benignity
Goodness
Longanimity
Mildness
Faith
Modesty
Continence
Chastity

Seven Capital Sins

Pride
Covetousness
Lust
Anger
Gluttony
Envy
Sloth

Order of Mass

Gathering and Entrance Procession
Greeting
Opening Prayer
Prayer of Praise
Penitential Rite
Liturgy of the Word
    First Reading (usually from the Old Testament)
    Psalm Response
    Second Reading (usually from an epistle in the New Testament)
    Gospel
    Homily
Creed
Prayer of the Faithful
Liturgy of the Eucharist
    Preparation and Offering of the Gifts of Bread and Wine
    Preface Prayer of Praise and Thanksgiving
    Eucharistic Prayer (including words of consecration and concluding with the community's great AMEN)
    Communion Rite: Lord's Prayer, Sign of Peace, Communion, Meditation
Concluding Prayer
Blessing
Dismissal

Rite of Reconciliation for Individuals

(Penance, Confession)

Greeting from the Priest
Sign of the Cross
Scripture Passage
Confession of Sin
    Here, honestly confess the sins that have been part of your life. All serious matters should be included, as well as less serious things that are troublesome in your life with the Lord.
Advice and Spiritual Counseling
Penance
    The prayer or good work that you will be asked to take on is a sign of your sincere repentance.
Prayer of Sorrow and Contrition

Absolution
    The Priest places his hands on your head (or extends his right hand toward you) and prays these words of forgiveness:
    God, the Father of mercies, through the death and resurrection of his Son has reconciled the world to himself and sent the Holy Spirit among us for the forgiveness of sins; through the ministry of the Church may God give you pardon and peace, and I absolve you from your sins in the name of the Father, and of the Son, and of the Holy Spirit.
Prayer of Praise, such as:
    Priest: Give thanks to the Lord, for he is good.
    Response: His mercy endures forever.
Dismissal, such as:
    The Lord has freed you from your sins. Go in peace.

Responsibilities for Catholics

The Great Commandment

"You shall love the Lord your God with all your heart, with all your soul, and with all your mind. You shall love your neighbor as yourself" (Mt 22:37-39).

The Ten Commandments (*cf. Ex 20; Chapter 15 of* Invitation)

1. I am the Lord your God. You shall honor no other god but me.
2. You shall not misuse the name of the Lord, your God.
3. You shall keep holy the Sabbath.
4. You shall honor your father and mother.
5. You shall not kill.
6. You shall not commit adultery.
7. You shall not steal.
8. You shall not bear false witness against your neighbor.
9. You shall not covet your neighbor's wife.
10. You shall not covet your neighbor's goods.

The Beatitudes (*Mt 5; cf. Chapter 15 of* Invitation)

1. Blessed are the poor in spirit; the reign of God is theirs.
2. Blessed are the sorrowing; they shall be consoled.
3. Blessed are the lowly; they shall inherit the land.
4. Blessed are they who hunger and thirst for holiness; they shall have their fill.
5. Blessed are they who show mercy; mercy shall be theirs.
6. Blessed are the single-hearted; they shall see God.
7. Blessed are the peacemakers; they shall be called sons of God.

8. Blessed are those persecuted for holiness' sake; the reign of God is theirs.

Spiritual Works of Mercy

To admonish the sinner
To instruct the ignorant
To counsel the doubtful
To comfort the sorrowful
To bear wrongs patiently
To forgive all injuries
To pray for the living and the dead

Corporal Works of Mercy

To feed the hungry
To give drink to the thirsty
To clothe the naked
To visit the imprisoned
To shelter the homeless
To visit the sick
To bury the dead

Laws of the Church
(adapted from 1994 Catholic Almanac, *Our Sunday Visitor Publication Division)*

From time to time the church has listed certain specific duties of Catholics. Some duties expected of Catholic Christians today include the following (those traditionally named as precepts of the church are marked with *):
1. To keep holy the day of the Lord's resurrection: to worship God by participating in Mass every Sunday and holy day of obligation;* to avoid those activities that would hinder renewal of soul and body, e.g., needless work and business activities, unnecessary shopping.
2. To lead a sacramental life: to receive Holy Communion frequently and the sacrament of penance regularly; minimally, to receive the sacrament of penance at least once a year (annual confession is obligatory only if serious sin is involved*); minimally, to receive Holy Communion at least once a year during the Easter season, between the first Sunday of Lent and Trinity Sunday.*
3. To study Catholic teaching in preparation for the sacrament of confirmation, to be confirmed, and then to continue to study and advance the message of Jesus.
4. To observe the marriage laws of the church;* to give religious training (by example and word) to one's children; to use parish schools and religious education programs.
5. To strengthen and support the church:* one's own parish community and parish priests; the worldwide church and the Holy Father.
6. To do penance, including abstaining from meat and fasting from food on the appointed days.*

7. To join in the missionary spirit and apostolate of the church.

Holy Days of Obligation (in the United States)

January 1 — Solemnity of Mary, Mother of God
Ascension Thursday — 40 Days after Easter
August 15 — Feast of the Assumption
November 1 — All Saint's Day
December 8 — Feast of the Immaculate Conception
December 25 — Christmas Day

Effective Jan. 1, 1993, in the United States, the precept to attend Mass is suspended whenever the Solemnity of Mary (Jan. 1), the Assumption (Aug. 15) or All Saints (Nov. 1) falls on a Saturday or Monday.

Regulations for Fast and Abstinence

Fasting means giving up food or some kinds of food for a specified period of time. In church regulations, abstinence means giving up meat for certain times. (For many years, abstinence was required of Catholics every Friday, as a communal way of observing Friday as a day for special penance. U.S. Catholics from the age of 14 throughout life are obliged to abstain from meat on Ash Wednesday, the Fridays of Lent and Good Friday. Catholics are no longer required to abstain from meat each Friday, although they are expected to exercise some form of penance on that day, in remembrance of Jesus' death for us.)

Catholics are expected to fast from food and liquids (other than water and medicine) for one hour before receiving Holy Communion.

Certain days are also set aside as days of fast and abstinence for Catholics, when adults are expected to eat only minimum amounts of food, no meat, and nothing between meals at all. In the United States, Ash Wednesday and Good Friday are such days of fast and abstinence.

Becoming a Catholic

A person who feels called to membership in the Catholic Church should contact a local parish. There are people there who are ready to help as you listen for the leading of the Holy Spirit. A Catholic friend, neighbor, or family member will often be happy to accompany you on these first steps.

If you are already baptized:

It is the policy of the Catholic Church that persons who are already validly baptized in another Christian community are not rebaptized if they choose to join the

Catholic Church. Instead, they are received into full communion with the Catholic Church according to the following rite, confirmed, and then invited to participate in Eucharist for the first time with the Catholic Church.

Celebrant: N., of your own free will you have asked to be received into full communion with the Catholic Church. You have made your decision after careful thought under the guidance of the Holy Spirit. I now invite you to come forward with your sponsor and profess the Catholic faith in the presence of this community. This is the faith in which, for the first time, you will be one with us at the Eucharist table of the Lord Jesus, the sign of the Church's unity.

The candidate recites the Nicene Creed with the congregation, and then adds: I believe and profess all that the holy Catholic Church believes, teaches and proclaims to be revealed by God.

Celebrant: N., the Lord receives you into the Catholic Church. His loving kindness has led you here so that, in the unity of the Holy Spirit, you may have full communion with us in the faith you have professed in the presence of his family.

If you are not already baptized:

Adults who are not already baptized and who wish to join the Catholic Church will be initiated in stages in the midst of the community. The sacraments of baptism, confirmation and first Eucharist are the three sacraments of initiation which bring a person into full membership in the Catholic Church. Parish communities will pray and walk with a person along the faith journey.

INDEX

NOTES

NOTES

NOTES

NOTES

NOTES